EMPTY MOMENTS

E M P T Y

Cinema, Modernity, and Drift

LEO CHARNEY

M O M E N T S

Duke University Press   Durham and London 1998

© 1998 Duke University Press

All rights reserved

Printed in the United States of America on acid-free paper ∞

Typeset in Berkeley Medium by Tseng Information Systems, Inc.

Library of Congress Cataloging-in-Publication Data

appear on the last printed page of this book.

This book is for my parents
Maurice and Hanna Kurz Charney
and for their parents
Leopold and Frida Wolf Kurz
Benjamin and Sadie Stang Charney

Contents

Acknowledgments

This book was for the most part researched and written during two years at the University of Iowa. I am grateful to Dudley Andrew, director of the Institute for Cinema and Culture, and Rick Altman, head of the film studies division, for the stimulating and supportive environment that made my work possible. Carol Schrage's help and friendship were indispensable to my Iowa experience, as were the assistance and good humor of Chris Brenneman, Kathie Crow, and Jayne Lillig and the graciousness of John Finamore and Susan McLean when I lived in their home.

My friends and family have sustained and indulged me through years of wrestling with this material. I hope that Paul Charney, Nancy Cho, Adrienne Crew, Frank Derby, Lilly Derby, Ed Dimendberg, Gregg Flaxman, Jennifer Hirsch, Samantha Holland, Becky Isaacs, Shelley Stamp Lindsey, Mary Murrell, Lauren Rabinovitz, Rachel Schwartz, Don and Gloria Wiener, Renée Wiener, and Carina Yervasi will excuse the impersonality of this list. I am indebted to Dudley Andrew and Robert Sklar for their continuing support. Ken Wissoker encouraged this project and brought it to publication more successfully than I could have imagined; thanks also to Marc Brodsky, Paula Dragosh, and the book's wonderful readers, as well as to the University of California Press for permission to reprint material from my essay in *Cinema and the Invention of Modern Life*. My greatest debts occur in inverse proportion to a few words' ability to repay them. Emily Pachuta's high standards, strong convictions, shrewd advice, and commitment to the enjoyment of daily life have shaped the texture of my life for more years than either of us may want to recall. Vanessa Schwartz has been an indefatigable friend, an inexhaustible ally, and my strongest intellectual influence. As much as her pioneering work generated my own interest in representation and modernity, she has taught me even more about the rigors and pleasures of friendship. Finally, this book is for my parents, Maurice and Hanna Kurz Charney, whose unwavering love and support made it possible.

O N E

Drift

Watch it. There it goes. It's gone.

• • •

April 5, 1931. André Breton in a café.

I had just told Paul Eluard my night dream (the one about the hashish),
and we were about to finish interpreting it with his help—for he had
observed how I had spent most of my time the day before—when my
gaze met that of a young woman or girl, seated with a man a few steps
from us. I surveyed her from head to toe at my leisure, or perhaps it
was that suddenly I could no longer detach my gaze from her.

April 20, 1934. André Breton eats lunch.

At the height of the occultation of Venus by the moon (this occurrence
only supposed to happen once in the year), I was having lunch in a little
restaurant rather unfortunately situated near the entrance of a cemetery.

I keep trying to tell him that he can't fix a single moment, but he's been
talking to his astrologer again.

"Whether or not it results from the conjunction of Venus with Mars at a
particular place in the sky of my birth, I have all too often felt the bad
effects of discord in the very inside of love."

I have to stop watching this.

It's like one train wreck after another.

Breton's spending his whole life trying to find one great moment, and it's never going to happen.

Doesn't he see it?

• • •

In 1915, Alfred Wegener put forward the first version of what he called "drift theory" and what has come to be known as the theory of continental drift. "This is the starting point of displacement or drift theory," wrote Wegener in the fourth edition of *The Origin of Continents and Oceans*. "The basic 'obvious' supposition common to . . . permanence theory—that the relative position of the continents . . . has never altered—must be wrong. The continents must have shifted."[1] In the words appropriated by Marshall Berman for the title of his seminal book on modernity, Karl Marx defined modernity as "all that is solid melts into air."[2] Wegener sends us down a different but related path where we might say that in modernity all that is stable drifts into motion. Like Einstein's image of elastic and relative time, Wegener's vision of continental drift magnified in global terms the destabilizing of simple, stationary presence that marked modernity.

If the philosophy and criticism of modernity were preoccupied with the loss of presence, where can we go conceptually after acknowledging that presence irrevocably becomes absence? Once we have recognized that presence cannot coincide with itself, that sensation and cognition are always already alienated, that the body lives in self-segregation, are we left with no epistemological alternatives other than to repeat these premises again and again like a mantra? Is this all there is to say about the absence of presence as an experiential condition of modernity? As each present moment is remorselessly evacuated and deferred into the future, it opens up an empty space, an interval, that takes the place of a stable present. This potentially wasted space provides an opening to drift, to put the empty present to work not as a self-present identity or a self-present body but as a drift, an ungovernable, mercurial activity that takes empty presence for granted while maneuvering within and around it.

The experience that I call drift describes neither certain texts nor a certain mode of engagement but the general activity of living with the empty present, carrying it forward through time and space. This is why we must not consider drift either as one kind of experience or as a description of certain valorized texts—Roland Barthes, Anton Chekhov, Andy Warhol, Alain Resnais, Michelangelo Antonioni—but as the general condition of subjective experience in the loss of presence. The experience of drift allows us to imagine the empty present both as ontology—as an unbridgeable structure no less insurmountable than the vision of full presence it displaces—and as epistemology, a way of knowing, a category of experience, a pragmatic strategy, a negotiation of "room for maneuver," in Ross Chambers's phrase, between experience and presence.[3] Wegener, who was not a geologist, did not observe the continents shift. He studied maps—representations of the continents—and theorized on that basis that land masses "must have shifted."

The emergence of cinema at the end of the nineteenth century crystallized into one form of technology, narrative, and experience the attributes of modernity expressed across the board in other discourses and phenomena. In the techniques of cinema, the ephemeral moment became the engine of motion, the peak moment the spur for stimulation, the empty moment the site of spectatorship. If we cannot understand the birth of cinema without the culture of modernity, we also cannot conceive modernity's culture of moments, fragments, and absent presents without the intervention of cinema, which became a crucible and a memorial for modernity's diverse aspects. More exactly, cinema formed a nexus of two characteristic elements of the culture of modernity: an ontology of re-presentation and an epistemology of drift. The absence of tangible present moments gave rise to a culture of re-presentation in which experience was always already lost, accessible only through retrospective textualization. Re-presentation as a mode of experience took the form of drift, which transfigured empty presence into a new modern epistemology. Drift aimed to re-present the experience of vacancy, the lived sensation of empty moments, the consequence and corollary of empty moments.

Drift became a significant category of modern experience along two axes. In the common sense of directionless passivity, drift provided the background for modernity's shocking moments, surprising distractions, and overwhelming stimuli. Momentary sensations became startling as perceptual contrasts to the undifferentiated drift of everyday experience. This sense of drift was most familiarly dramatized in the plays and stories of Chekhov, who created a body of literature around the tragicomic inability of the Russian upper classes to battle a heritage of drift.[4] Chekhov's plays, and such fiction as the emblematically titled "A Boring Story," vividly dramatized the modern drive to put drift to work, to fight drift's seductive pull by replacing it with constructive labor. For Chekhov's characters, work symbolizes the new modern Russia to which they cannot or will not adapt, and inertia embodies the privileges to which they vainly cling. In *The Three Sisters,* the inability of the sisters to make their endlessly talked-about move to Moscow becomes as comic as the refusal of *The Cherry Orchard*'s Madame Ranevskaya to take action to save her doomed property. "Forgive me," Lopakhin explodes in act 2 of *The Cherry Orchard,* "but I have never seen such frivolous, such queer, unbusinesslike people as you, my friends. You are told in plain language that your estate is to be sold, and it's as though you don't understand it." Madame Ranevskaya characteristically responds, "But what are we to do? Tell us what to do," a remark that echoes Irina's distracted comment to Chebutykin in act 4 of *The Three Sisters,* "Yes, you really ought to change your life, my dear. You really should—somehow."

Throughout this play, Irina recognizes work as the solution to her passive drift: "Man must work . . . and in this alone lies the meaning and purpose of his life, his happiness, his ecstasy. . . . In the same way that one has a craving for water in hot weather, I have a craving for work. . . . We must work, work. That's why we're so melancholy and take such a gloomy view of life, because we know nothing of work. We come of people who despised work." Irina's rhetorical paeans to work are almost identical to those of Trofimov in *The Cherry Orchard*, who orates in act 2: "Everything that is now unattainable will some day be comprehensible and within our grasp, only we must work. . . . The great majority of the intelligentsia that I know seek nothing, do nothing, and as yet are incapable of work. . . . all our fine talk is merely to delude ourselves and others. . . . to begin to live we must first atone for the past, be done with it, and we can atone for it only by suffering, only by extraordinary, unceasing labor."

Chekhov's characters talk a good game about shaking off drift, but as Irina recognizes in the unbearably sad third act of *The Three Sisters*, "life is slipping by, never to return, never, we shall never go to Moscow. I see that we shall never go." The effort to combat lethargy through work cannot fight the allure of drift, in which, as Madame Ranevskaya puts it in act 3 of *The Cherry Orchard*, "you do nothing, fate simply tosses you from place to place—it's so strange." For Lopakhin, who will symbolically take over Ranevskaya's estate, the pull of drift is both alien and pernicious: "I've been hanging around here with you, and I'm sick and tired of loafing. I can't live without work, I don't know what to do with my hands." As the play's symbolism makes clear, Lopakhin's nonrhetorical devotion to work epitomizes the modern movement away from indolent upper-class drift. Though his outburst arises as much from infatuation as from principle, Astrov in *Uncle Vanya* says the same thing in exploding at Elena in act 4: "Both of you—he and you—have infected us with your idleness. I was infatuated with you and have done nothing for a whole month; . . . wherever you set foot, you and your husband, you bring ruin."

Yet drift could also name the activity that battled empty presence by appropriating it, maneuvering within and around it. This form of drift was emblematized in the work of another avatar of the literature of modernity, Marcel Proust. The opening pages of the opening section of the opening part of *A la recherche du temps perdu* articulate the paradigmatic account of modern drift as a state of consciousness collapsed into a mode of re-presentation. These pages proffer a description of drift and a polemic for drift, as well as a drifting meditation on drift. These passages, in which Proust's narrator ambivalently drifts off to and around sleep, set the tone for the whole work in joining the content of drift to the form of drift. "For a long time I used to go to bed early," Proust's narrator begins, so that the text in beginning is already superficially closing.[5] But this gesture remains more complicated, since Proust raises going to bed to the level of epistemology—or, rather, the narrator's bed becomes the site of the epistemology of drift. Drift appears not as an antiepistemology, a rejection of or rebellion against epistemology, but as a specific way to grasp and re-present experience. This is the innovation of Proust's expression of drift: it is not that the experiences described are experiences *of* drift—drift as ontology—but that the oblique approach toward them manifests drift as an epistemological process, a strategy of knowing the thing rather than the thing itself.

Yet Proust's logic of drift must by definition place in question this attractively schematic distinction. *A la recherche*'s massively redundant brief for subjectivity can hardly be said to have its insidious impact—its effect of seeping into your bloodstream, as in the work of such other artists of drift as Agnes Martin, Barthes, and Antonioni—if we can still deploy the concept of the "thing itself" segregated from how it is known: re-membered, re-constructed, re-presented. From the start in Proust, the logic of drift is a logic of subjectivity as and at an extreme. Closeted in his bed in his room, Proust drifts through a universe of events, all of them functions of his rigorously total subjectivity, subjectivity functioning so wholly as epistemology as to transform epistemology into ontology.

Proust's strategic drift, as it stretches across the first pages of *Swann's Way*, provides the paradigm for the modern category of drift in that it is never simply a forward stream but rather an erratic vagrancy, a structured wandering. Proust's drift is a bumpy ride. "Sometimes," the narrator tells us in the second sentence, he falls asleep right away, "so quickly that I didn't have time to say to myself, 'I'm falling asleep.'" But even in those cases, the third sentence reports, a half-hour would not pass before he would be up again, tormented by thoughts about sleep so winding as to prevent sleep itself. The narrator's ambivalence and his commitment to the subjective purity of his reveries are both so radically total as to extend to each of the day's twenty-four hours. The category of "sleep" becomes a vague social convention in the face of such a thorough-going immersion in subjective experience and/as drift. The day's twenty-four hours form one experience—the experience of drift—that supersedes a simple segregation of experience into sleep and nonsleep.

The austerity of Proust's adherence to subjectivity and drift arises from this effacement of the boundary between sleep experience and nonsleep experience. In the first pages of *Swann's Way*, sleep becomes the analogue of drift, or, more exactly, the site of drift. "Sleep" as a state of experience is replaced by drift, which weaves sleep and nonsleep into one continuous experience as it brings together past and present. He prefers a heavy sleep, Proust's narrator tells us, because

> it loosened my grip on the place where I had fallen asleep and, when I woke up in the middle of the night, as I did not know where I was, I did not even know for the first instant who I was; . . . but then the memory—not yet of the place where I was, but of some of the places where I had lived or where I could have been—came to me like help from on high to pull me out of the nothingness which I could not have left all alone; in one second I would pass through centuries of civilization.

This passage, like others in Proust, makes clear that drift is not even and durational but studded with instantaneous flashes of consciousness and perception: "I did not even know for the first instant who I was"; "in one second I would pass through centuries of civilization"; or, two paragraphs earlier and most explicit, "I would fall asleep again, and sometimes I would wake up only for short instants . . . to taste thanks to a flash of consciousness the sleep into which were plunged the furniture, the room, everything of which I was only a small part and whose unconsciousness I was quickly rejoining." These momentary sparks occupy a symbiotic relationship to the drift with which they coexist: momentary instants can be recognized only in contrast to the more undifferentiated drift that surrounds and contains them; from the other side, we conceptualize drift as the contrasting form of experience to the intense instants, the sublime or ecstatic moments that set it off. As Richard Goodkin suggests, this interplay between the continuous and the momentary characterizes Proust's drift as both content and form; Proust's wandering sentences—the form of drift—take their shape from the failed effort to encapsulate the sensations of a discrete moment.

Proust's notoriously long and convoluted sentences create the impression of a Zenonian chase. Not only do they often take place within a single moment of time, but they also seem unable to come to a close precisely because they cannot manage to circumscribe what they are quite literally talking "about." The Proustian sentence gives the impression of an infinite narration of a single moment, of an unremitting postponement of the arrival at a goal (the end of the sentence), of a dissatisfaction arising both from the unrepresentability of a single moment and from the unpleasant feeling that no moment ever really "leads" to another moment except by default, or perhaps exhaustion.[6]

As Proust exemplifies, the instants do not occur separately from drift, and it is not quite the point to say that they form part of drift. They are the drift. Drift constitutes not an even, forward flow but a mercurial and variable experience, diffuse and distracted, unquantifiable. In Proust's exhaustive textualization of experience, the logic of drift subsumes even—especially—the sensations of discrete moments. Individual moments occur like buoys bobbing on the surface of drift: they cannot stop or alter drift; they participate in it, are pulled along by it, set themselves off against it.

Proust thereby compels us to consider the centrality of drift even to visions of modernity as fugitive and momentary. We are familiar with a vision of urban modernity in the late nineteenth and early twentieth centuries as an experience of short sharp shocks: in the words of Georg Simmel in 1903, "the rapid crowding of changing images, the sharp discontinuity in the grasp of a single glance, and the unexpectedness of onrushing impressions."[7] We need not eradicate this view to understand its dialectical relation to drift, which must retake its place as an equally vital category of modern consciousness.

• • •

Everyone says modern life, coming out of the late nineteenth and early twentieth centuries, was about too much happening, things moving too fast, assaulting you, too much stimulation, too many distractions. Simmel in 1903: "With each crossing of the street," the city dweller is accosted by "the rapid crowding of changing images, the sharp discontinuity in the grasp of a single glance, and the unexpectedness of onrushing impressions."

But they have it backward.

Modernity's about the emptiness, the drift.

All those things going on were a cover, to mask the emptiness.

Once people realized life was empty and boring, they couldn't face it.

They had to have all those things going on to make them forget, to deny it, make it go away, go back to a time before they knew that life was empty and boring.

And to make it seem like it wasn't.

This is the history of television.

• • •

Gilles Deleuze wrote in *The Logic of Sense* that in Stoic philosophy, there are two kinds of time, "one of which is composed only of interlocking presents; the other is constantly decomposed into elongated pasts and futures."

Time is either all presents or no presents.

There is either one present moment after another after another or no present moment at all, only past barreling through what we call present into what we call future.

We know there's no present, so he's half-right.

But there also isn't no present.

There's the empty present, a space in place of the present.

The present goes away and leaves behind an empty space.

Why do people assume it stays vacant.

Nature abhors a vacuum.

• • •

Edmund Husserl says that the first moment when the body gets the sensation, before we recognize or react to it, is the one way the present can happen.

He calls it the "pure now."

When I hit my toe, it's right there, in that moment.

And it's the only thing that can ever be right there, inside a moment.

One problem.

There's no way to know it.

We have to assume there's a moment of pure body sensation before the mind butts in, but by definition we can't know that it's there.

You can feel how he wants it both ways.

He calls the present a "fantasy."

He calls it "presentification," meaning it's something we make up, a construction.

Then he says the first moment when the body receives the sensation can be "an ideal limit, something abstract which can be nothing for itself."

Which is it?

• • •

The body receives a sensation in that "pure now."

It's a "limit" because it draws the boundaries of the possibility of a present moment.

And it's "ideal" because it's imaginary, because we can never know that it happens. We have to assume it does. It's there, but we can't know it's there. We have to take Husserl's word for it.

You see how it makes him nervous to say there's no present.

He needs to keep a floor below the abyss.   ,

But what if there's no floor.

What if we're all just falling.

• • •

Absolute Waste

The modern epistemology of lost and wasted presence from which drift arose first emerged in 1852, when Sir William Thomson, later known as Lord Kelvin, published his elliptically apocalyptic statement "On a Universal Tendency in Nature to the Dissipation of Mechanical Energy."[8] This essay, which articulated what came to be called Kelvin's laws of thermodynamics, began with a statement breathtaking in its acceptance of loss: "The object of the present communication is to call attention to the remarkable consequences which follow from Carnot's proposition, that there is an absolute waste of mechanical energy available to man when heat is allowed to pass from one body to another" (511). Thomson's devastating phrase "absolute waste" imagines a waste both all-encompassing and inescapable, more certain and despairing than simple waste.

Thomson's waste generates from the paradox that heat can be produced only by wasting heat. This is for modernity an emblematic conundrum, which Thomson foreshadowed at midcentury: the mechanism that creates heat also dissipates heat, and this dissipation, Thomson hastened to note in case we expected a silver lining, is unrecoverable. The permanent vacation of heat was expressed straightforwardly in the second law of thermodynamics: "Any restoration of mechanical energy, without more than an equivalent of dissipation, is impossible" (514). Here again Thomson insisted on waste's inescapability: even the futile effort at restoration could occur only if, two steps forward and three steps back, it would dissipate heat all over again. In the earlier section of this brief essay, Thomson, like an insistent prosecutor, hammered this point again and again, rhythmically repeating three times, in three different examples of heat transference, "a full restoration of it to its primitive condition is impossible," then "perfect restoration is impossible," and, again, "perfect restoration is impossible" (512).

The focus on impossibility, imperfection, negativity, waste, and loss would in itself anticipate modernity's gloomy spirit. But the wider framework of Thomson's argument—and its aspect that has caused the most controversy and dissension[9]—is its forecast of apocalypse. For if every exchange that creates heat must also waste heat, there will eventually be no heat left. It will all have been wasted, dissipated, pointlessly evaporated. Thomson expressed this idea in the essay's last sentence, his third law, put soberly yet in a winding manner almost Proustian in form:

> Within a finite period of time past, the earth must have been, and within a finite period to come the earth must again be, unfit for the habitation of man as at present constituted, unless operations have been, or are to be performed, which are impossible under the laws to which the known operations going on at present in the material world are subject. (514)

In other words, it would be possible if it were not impossible. Thomson's bleak stoicism, partially masked by the cheery scientism of his language, posited loss and waste as metonyms of apocalypse. Each combination of objects that creates heat—friction is Thomson's favorite example—wastes heat in the service of the final apocalypse of heat, when only cold will remain.

Thomson's vision of wasted heat marked a potent metaphor for modernity in its insistence on both the prevalence of waste and its unrecoverability. All positive action is predicated on loss, which is unrecoverable and unredeemable, "absolute waste." Yet he argued not simply that waste and loss surround us like vultures but also that they occur as the output of two bodies that come together. The encounter of two bodies produces (1) a new, third body in some way different from the sum of the two parts and (2) the wasted energy needed to create this third element. What came to be known as Kelvin's thermodynamics thereby indicated how waste that might seem "absolute" in the long run can nevertheless forge extra space that could compose a parallel track around presence. Thomson's innovation was to gesture outside presence, drawing our attention to the waste and the loss that subvert yet make possible simple presence. In so doing, he anticipated the means by which empty presence could be recouped, even as he set forward the terms of empty presence that would preoccupy thinkers in modernity.

For instance, in *Looking Backward: 2000–1887*, a fantasy of how the late nineteenth century would look from the perspective of the millennium, Edward Bellamy suggested that modernity's waste and inefficiency would seem preposterous from the perspective of an efficiently industrialized future. Bellamy indicated modernity's waste and inertia on almost every page, leading up to the climactic list:

> First, the waste by mistaken undertakings; second, the waste from the competition and mutual hostility of those engaged in industry; third, the waste by periodical gluts and crises, with the consequent interruptions of industry; fourth, the waste from idle capital and labor, at all times. Any one of these four great leaks, were all the others stopped, would suffice to make the difference between wealth and poverty on the part of a nation.[10]

Bellamy's damning perspective on the wastes of modernity relied on the presumption that waste was neither natural nor inevitable but could be mitigated by thrift, thought, and hard work. As Cecelia Tichi notes, while for Bellamy "waste is the culprit in all human suffering, . . . a state of waste is not immutable. It is susceptible to correction in the achievement of its contrary, efficiency. Coupled with that contrary, 'waste' invites, in fact demands, corrective action. In denotation and connotation the word is a summons to it."[11] Bellamy did not simply posit work as the antidote to waste but began to indicate how work and waste could exist only in a mutually defining pas de deux. This interlacing of work and waste reflected the similar symbiosis between the momentary and the continuous; more important, it occurred against the background of drift, work's seeming opposite, which clarified by contrast the need for productive work.

Yet drift could itself be articulated as a new modern means of putting waste to work. Drift as epistemology describes the mercurial yet strategic form of wandering that arose from the culture of empty presence and emerged as the form of film spectatorship. The logic of drift meanders, digresses, floats; in Barthes's memorable words, drift "occurs whenever I do not respect the whole, and whenever . . . I remain motionless, pivoting on the intractable bliss that binds me to the text (to the world). . . . Thus another name for drifting would be: the Intractable—or perhaps even: Stupidity."[12] Barthes's vision of drift as mobile nothingness occurs not as a function of the text but as a rebellion against it, on the side of individual pleasure: "Pleasure, however, is not an element of the text, it is not a naïve residue; it does not depend on a logic of understanding and on sensation; it is a drift, something both revolutionary and asocial, and it cannot be taken over by any collectivity, any mentality, any ideolect" (23). Yet in the spirit of Barthes's conception, we must in turn resist the impulse to pin drift simply to pleasure, a strategy that remakes drift straightforwardly readable: in coinciding with something called "pleasure," drift restores the possibility of self-coincidence that it must instead struggle to undermine. What drift does, to the extent that it does anything, is get beyond the fetishization of the present, of presence, of the single moment. As Jürgen Habermas said of modernity, "The new value placed on the transitory, the elusive, and the ephemeral, the very celebration of dynamism, discloses the longing for an undefiled, an immaculate and stable present."[13] Drift unmoors our fixation from the single empty present and sends us out into a fluid, mobile, bodily activity.

The logic of drift faces up to the death of presence not by relegating presence to the irrational body and to the status of speculation but by collapsing the possibility of presence into a logic of representation that becomes a variable subjectivity, a mobilized epistemology. More exactly, we could fill out Habermas's generalization by suggesting that Husserl, Henri Bergson, and Martin Heidegger all recuperated presence through two strategies: assigning it to the irrational feelings of the body while removing it from the rational or cognitive realm; and thereby presenting the present as speculative, as an unknowable hypothetical limit that nevertheless keeps a lid on the ungovernable potential of absence.

On the one hand, Husserl called presence a "fantasy" (a term that still allowed it to exist) and offered in its place the useful term "presentification."[14] Presence can occur, this term reminds us, only as a fabrication, a fiction. Yet despite this bracing rigor in eviscerating presence, Husserl opened the door for what he called the "self-giving of the actual present." The "actual present"—the only form of a present that can actually occur—gives itself to itself; it does not reach outside itself but simply (and that is the word) feels a sensation inside the present moment. This is a present that belongs wholly to the body and its sensations. "In an ideal sense, then," Husserl put it, "perception (impression) would be the phase of consciousness which constitutes the pure now, and memory every other phase of the continuity" (63). What we call the "presence" of a sensation is actually the memory of the "pure" present once felt by the body.

This possibility of the self-giving present seems enmeshed in a logical paradox. Presence can exist, but only in a form that ensures that we cannot know it to exist. How, then, do we know that it occurs? More important, why do we still need a concept of presence at all? In spite of his overwhelming supposition to the contrary, Husserl keeps presence in place as the floor below the abyss. He says this more or less explicitly, calling presence "just an ideal limit, something abstract which can be nothing for itself" (63). The hypothetical possibility of presence places a limit on how bottomlessly the void of nonpresence can fall. When Husserl calls this cardboard cutout version of presence "ideal," he veers perilously close to Habermas's critique of "the longing for an undefiled, an immaculate and stable present."

In similar fashion, Heidegger proposed that in the moment of vision we experience a direct sensation that we can grasp in the immediacy of a present presence: "The moment of vision," he wrote in *Being and Time,* "permits us to encounter for the first time what can be 'in a time' as ready-to-hand or present-at-hand." [15] In the moment of vision, we "encounter" sensation in the practical realm that Heidegger called the "ready-to-hand or present-at-hand." We experience the moment of vision in a nonrational way, and this experience fills us with the ecstatic sensation of being present inside the present. Heidegger's view allowed the present to occur, but only as a bodily sensation thereby marked as irrational: the moment of vision "must be understood in the active sense as an ecstasis. It means the resolute rapture with which *Dasein* [the subject] is carried away to whatever possibilities and circumstances are encountered in the Situation" (387).

In becoming drift, re-presentation emerges as not just an ontology, a hypothetical philosophical tenet, but an epistemology, a modern means of grasping experience—both by failing to grasp it and by acknowledging the inescapability of that failure. The epistemology of drift takes for granted the circling indirection of representation, and this floating inexactness becomes the only way to know my own or any other experience. More to the point, drift occurs in the unquantifiable physiological realm opened up by the putative split between a bodily moment of presence and the cognitive moments that follow in its wake. If we cannot identify the present moment inside the present moment, "presence" splits into two tracks: the recognition, located in the mind, of presence as presence; and an anarchic mystery zone, located in the body, in which the "actual" presence of sensations and perceptions is presumed to occur. This presence is by definition imaginary, a "hypothetical limit." Presence occurs in the body before and in the absence of cognitive recognition, so that it must always occur as a supposition, an after-the-fact discursive construction.

The body in this way became a potentially anarchic and essentially split organism, functioning partly in the sun of cognition and partly in a shadow realm of sensation. In this shady sensual underworld, perceptions passing through the body spin off into an apocalypse of loss—unknowable, never knowable. The space between what the body receives sensually and what it processes cognitively gives corporeal form to the conceptions of wasted space and empty presence that threaded their way through philosophy, aesthetics, psychology, and science in this period. The segregation of the body provides a fictional means to continue to figure a present moment that can never be known and must be taken on faith. Yet while the figuration of this hypothetical bodily netherworld is to some extent an opportunistic gesture to rescue presence, it also opens up a parallel track around presence. This unknown and unknowable realm locates the errant vagrancy of drift, the limit of a discourse of presence transfigured as subjectivity. Drift maneuvers around presence; it is not subsumed by the possibility of presence or by the stasis of a single present moment. Drift wanders, but the wandering does not wander away from a stable linear order that grounds it: the wandering is the thing itself.

• • •

"Without language, thought is a vague, uncharted nebula. . . . our thought
—apart from its expression in words—is only a shapeless and indistinct mass."—Ferdinand de Saussure

I've got news for you: sometimes it's a shapeless and indistinct mass anyway.

Control.

Everyone wants it.

It's what everything's finally about.

Control things hard enough and maybe you can control death too.

But it could be so much easier.

The answer's right in front of you.

There it is. There it was. There it is again.

Let it control you.

Let yourself drift.

That's how you slip inside the empty moment.

• • •

It doesn't make sense. Logically.

You'd think you'd have to stop time just to keep up.

That's what makes the mechanism inexplicable.

How do you do it without losing a step?

Without slipping? Without losing your footing once in a while?

Without getting backlogged like a harassed file clerk?

How does it fail to happen?

• • •

So you can sympathize with Husserl and Heidegger and Bergson and all
the people who can't let go of presence.

It's a clutter, it defies explanation, so they want to hang on to something
they can grasp.

The moment of vision "must be understood in the active sense as an ecstasis. It means the resolute rapture with which Dasein is carried away to

21

whatever possibilities and circumstances are encountered in the Situation."

Whatever.

But there is no moment of vision.

Heidegger thinks he can get around this by calling it ecstatic, making it irrational.

The moment of vision carried you away.

You couldn't help it.

You tried to say no.

You were overcome by the rapture.

You were too weak to resist.

· · ·

Heidegger calls it the moment of vision, Husserl calls it the ideal limit.

Either way it's a present.

No matter how much they qualify and hedge, it's still a present.

Why do they need so desperately to hang on to presence?

Why do they still need a concept of presence?

You see how they do it.

They position presence inside the split between the body and the mind.

A split they have created and reinforced.

In *Matter and Memory,* Bergson does it too:

> My present consists in the consciousness I have of my body. . . . More generally, in that continuity of becoming which is reality itself, the present moment is constituted by the quasi-instantaneous section effected by our perception in the flowing mass, and this section is precisely that which we call the material world. Our body occupies its center; it is, in this material world, that part of which we directly feel the flux; in its actual state the actuality of our present lies. . . . our present is the very materiality of our existence, that is to say, a system of sensations and movements and nothing else.

· · ·

It's just the body.

Who cares what happens there.

We can't figure out what happens in there anyway.

It might as well be a present.

There's no way to prove it.

Who'll know the difference?

Who'll argue otherwise.

        •   •   •

For Husserl and for Bergson and for Heidegger, the body becomes a scrap
heap of lost presents.

Presence exists, but only in a form that ensures we cannot ever know it
to exist.

That's a great system.

There is no present—except that the pathetic, deluded body doesn't know
it yet.

Sssh.

Don't tell it.

        •   •   •

I move. I put my foot forward.

But it's already happened.

My body performed the action in advance.

What happens in the body is no more and no less present.

It just happens first.

These philosophies depend on keeping the body in the dark.

They need an ignorant body.

They're not totally wrong. It's the emphasis that's wrong.

We all know there's no link between the body and the mind.

The body is a wild shadow realm.

It's out there on its own.

        •   •   •

They have it precisely backward.

They got it unerringly and exactly wrong.

The body locates not the site of presence but a parallel track around what you call presence.

The body finalizes the impossibility of stable presence.

You can't privilege the body as the site either of presence or of nonpresence.

Like presence, the body drifts.

• • •

Between presence and nonpresence, between body and mind, between the strictly positive and the strictly negative — between any rigid polarity — drift intervenes.

Drift is the experience of the empty present, the empty present rendered as experience.

Drift is how the empty present makes itself felt.

To you.

Drift is as close as you get to feeling the empty present.

• • •

People ask me: how does it feel to drift.

What they mean is: how does the empty moment feel.

What they mean is: how can I know how the empty moment would feel.

I tell them they can't know.

It's like asking how it feels to be dead.

You can't imagine it.

You're locked into presence.

By definition you can't conceive a whole different foundation for your experience.

• • •

Thomson makes sure we can't miss the point:
"a full restoration . . . is impossible"

"perfect restoration is impossible"
"perfect restoration is impossible"
He repeats it over and over again like a mantra.
A mantra of waste and futility.
Of total loss.
The mantra of modernity.

. . .

People focus on death—linear, lucid, graspable, absolute—instead of on
the death that inhabits every minute of their life.

They object to Thomson's saying there will—someday, one day, who
knows when, maybe the earth won't even exist any longer—be no heat,
and they miss his real point: everything's gone, wasted, lost. We can't
get it back.

Each moment is haunted by emptiness and pointlessness. Not by choice
or by temperament. That's the way it is.

Thomson opens up the space of drift.

He shows us the parallel track around presence.

And documents that the same mechanics that produce presence also produce its shadow of waste.

This is the space in which you can drift.

. . .

25

T W O

The Present Moment

In a posthumously published essay, Virginia Woolf sketched a scene she called "The Moment: Summer's Night."[1] She began with five sentences that described the environment around her, from murmuring trees to an airplane hum "like a piece of plucked wire" to "the distant explosion of a motor cycle, shooting further and further away down the road" (3). Having filled in these details that combined a rustic pastoral vision with the foreboding echoes of modernity, Woolf stopped to ponder:

> Yet what composed the present moment? If you are young, the future lies upon the present, like a piece of glass, making it tremble and quiver. If you are old, the past lies upon the present, like a thick glass, making it waver, distorting it. All the same, everybody believes that the present is something, seeks out the different elements in this situation in order to compose the truth of it, the whole of it. (3)

Woolf's brief excursion into articulating her tactile sense of the moment provides apt introduction to how the moment's characteristics were conceived in this period. "To begin with," Woolf noted, the present moment "is largely composed of visual and of sense impressions" (3). To describe how the moment is defined visually and sensually, Woolf deployed the concept of the "impression." Her brief essay consists almost entirely of impressionistic descriptions of the visions and feelings around her. Yet Woolf's nostalgically retrospective tone embodies the realization that the moment, by nature fleeting, can be (re)constructed only after the fact.

In this way, Woolf sketched a central philosophical problem of modernity: If our sensation and perception tell us that a moment of presence is possible—because we can feel it—how can this possibility be reconciled with the impossibility of stopping or doubling back in time? The possibility of a moment opens a hole in time, a chasm between the sensation of the moment, which can occur in the moment, and the rational effort to recognize, classify, or respond to that sensation, which can arise only after the moment and while other moments are still occurring behind it. The simple single moment was conceived as inconceivable both because the moment is always already gone before we can perceive it and because the single moment is therefore extended beyond one moment. "Let any one try," wrote William James in his 1890 *Principles of Psychology,* "I will not say to arrest, but to notice or attend to, the present moment of time. One of the most baffling experiences occurs. Where is it, this present? It has melted in our grasp, fled ere we could touch it, gone in the instant of becoming."[2]

For such emblematic modern philosophers as Edmund Husserl and Martin Heidegger, the "falling into lostness," as Heidegger called it, created by the inability to occupy a present moment characterized the alienation of modern experience. The modern subject was inexorably split between the body's sensations, which occurred in one moment, and the consciousness of those sensations, which could not be present in that same moment. He or she was thereby primordially alienated from the responses and impressions of his or her own body. This breach could be redeemed—although it was more a capitulation than a redemption—only by succumbing to what Heidegger called the "resolute rapture with which *Dasein* [the subject] is carried away" by instants of noncognitive feeling and sensation.[3] The immediate, sensual reality of vision or sensation could in fact occur inside a moment. The crucial conceptual leap lies in recognizing and acknowledging that cognition does not define the entire possibility of presence. If we cannot feel and perceive the moment in the same moment, that inability does not mean that no present presence can occur: it simply means that we can only feel it. In a moment, the body receives sensation nonrationally—or, more exactly, prerationally. By the time cognition catches up to sensation, the moment is gone.

The modern reconception of presence that emerged out of late-nineteenth-century psychology to become the dominant theme of early-twentieth-century philosophy focused on the notion that what we consider a "moment" of presence must in fact be composed of several moments. In *Principles of Psychology*, James called this problem that of the "specious present." Although in theory the present would be momentary, the present "moment" that we perceive in practice extends longer than one instant. This distension of the present was demonstrated, as James noted, in the nineteenth-century research of such psychologists as Wilhelm Wundt and Georg Dietze, whose work suggested the maximum and minimum amounts of time, measured in seconds, that frame what we perceive as a moment. "The specious present," James summarized these findings, "has, in addition, a vaguely vanishing backward and forward fringe; but its nucleus is probably the dozen seconds or less that have just elapsed."[4]

In the philosophical realm, the extension of presence is more familiar from Heidegger's Saussurean principle of "seeing-as." "When we have to do with anything," Heidegger wrote in *Being and Time*, "the mere seeing of the Things which are closest to us bears in itself the structure of interpretation. . . . In dealing with what is environmentally ready-to-hand. . . , we 'see' it *as* a table, a door, a carriage, or a bridge. . . . Any mere . . . seeing of the ready-to-hand is, in itself, something which already understands and interprets" (190, 189). Although we appear to recognize worldly phenomena instantaneously, the visual awareness and the ascription of meaning cannot occur in the same moment. Even the most rudimentary perceptions are denied the solace of simple presence.

This division of the present moment into stages was pioneered by Heidegger's mentor Husserl, who straightforwardly called presence a "fantasy."[5] Husserl rejected the concept of presence in favor of what he called "presentification." Presence, this neologism indicates, can be conceived only as a fabrication, a fiction. The possibility of presence can happen in two registers: a pure present of raw sensation that occurs before and in the absence of the mind's endeavor to categorize it "as" something; and then the "running-off" process in which efforts to account for that presence move further and further away from the initial generative presence. In this "running-off," the construction of something we call "present" becomes a function of increasingly distant memory. The fabrication of presence moves further into the future as the moment of presence moves further into the past.

Husserl called the moment of perceptual presence "the self-giving of the actual present" (63), "self-giving" in that it exists in the absence of meaning imposed on it after the fact. This moment constitutes the only real "presence" and immediately becomes past: "In an ideal sense, then," Husserl put it, "perception (impression) would be the phase of consciousness which constitutes the pure now, and memory every other phase of the continuity" (63). This possibility remains not just self-giving but self-denying, in that it represents a hypothetical horizon, "just an ideal limit, something abstract which can be nothing for itself" (63). The moment of impression in which sensation hits the body "can be nothing" in itself, yet this nothing is the tragic everything of presence. We can construe presence only as it becomes past. "Since a new now is always presenting itself, each now is changed into a past, and thus the entire continuity of the running-off of the pasts of the preceding points moves uniformly 'downward' into the depths of the past" (50).

In Husserl's model, the present occurs not just as a compound of moments of sensation and cognition but as "a single continuum which is constantly modified" (62) as it moves away from the perceptual present. The moment is inherently continuous; it can occur only as a span across memory, in the series of moments Husserl called "running-off." The "now" wanes in strength, moment by moment, as it passes into the future and becomes more and more past. This process forces us to split the general sense of "memory" into two forms. What we usually call "memory" becomes for Husserl "secondary remembrance or recollection" (57). The recollection of something truly past is distinguished from "primary remembrance," the form of memory that constructs immediate presence. Primary remembrance, which could be called "retention," was figured by Husserl as "a comet's tail which is joined to actual perception" (57). The attribution of memory/meaning trails in the wake of the moment of perception, getting thinner and thinner as it gets progressively more distant from its source.

• • •

Saussure was saying last night that the problem with movies is there's too much going on.

He can't get used to it.

He can't keep up.

That's the point, I tried to tell him.

Trying to make sense of a movie is like trying to make the present present.

You can't stop it, you can't keep pace, more and more keeps happening, there's more in each moment than you can take in, and that moment's already gone, and you have to keep up the best you can. You make meaning out of whatever you can salvage from all the waste and excess and mess.

And it all just generates more and more waste.

I don't think he appreciated it.

• • •

With so much going on, watching a movie could be like scaling a cliff with no footholds.

The empty moment gives the viewer a foot in the door of the runaway train.

A film's open spaces call out to us like beacons in the night; they pull the viewer in and give the viewer a place.

33

Because the film is disjointed and incomplete, it leaves room for us to enter.

Because it's a grab bag of fragments, we have to fill it out, paste together the broken pieces.

Because a film's act of re-presentation can never close in on itself, it needs us, wants us, reaches out to us.

The empty moment becomes a film's enabling loophole.

A film puts the empty moment to work.

• • •

The Artistic Moment

The idea that art relied on the representation of privileged moments did not, of course, originate in the nineteenth-century surge of photography and photographic arts. Most famously, Gotthold Lessing, in his 1766 *Laocoön*, posited that painting and sculpture would always be limited by their restriction to one temporal moment. That moment must therefore be as suggestive as possible:

> If the artist can never make use of more than a single moment in ever-changing nature, and if the painter in particular can use this moment only with reference to a single vantage point, while the works of both painter and sculptor are created not merely to be given a glance but to be contemplated—contemplated repeatedly and at length—then it is evident that the single moment and the point from which it is viewed cannot be chosen with too great a regard for its effect.[6]

Lessing already conceived the single represented moment as spilling beyond one moment. The moment, he specified, is designed "not merely to be given a glance but to be . . . contemplated repeatedly and at length." For this reason, the moment must leave space for the play of the viewer's imagination. The artist should never represent a moment of peak emotion, since "to present the utmost to the eye is to bind the wings of fancy and compel it" (19). The re-presentation of a peak emotion does not allow the viewer to imagine that emotional climax, and without that space for spectatorial imagination, the picture will lose its effect. In this way, momentary representation relies on the perceptual extension of the single moment. And this distension occurs through the structural use of empty space, which the picture opens up for the viewer's creative participation.

This notion of the artistic extension of the moment was picked up some 150 years later—and therefore in the context of photography—by Auguste Rodin, who suggested that his sculptures, in expressing the evolution of gestures across time, were therefore more "realistic" than the artificially paralyzed representations of photographs. Figures in photographs, said Rodin in his published conversations with Paul Gsell, "present the bizarre appearance of a man suddenly struck with paralysis and petrified in his pose . . . there is not, as in art, the gradual unfolding of movement." When Gsell objected that therefore the artist "evidently alters the truth" because photography must be considered an "unimpeachable mechanical witness" to human movement, Rodin responded that the reverse is the case: "It is the artist who tells the truth and photography that lies. For in reality, time does not stand still. And if the artist succeeds in producing the impression of a gesture that is executed in several instants, his work is certainly much less conventional than the scientific image where time is abruptly suspended."[7] Rodin believed that his quasi-photographic sculpture could more faithfully reflect the nature of the moment, in which what we perceive as one moment plays out across a series of moments.

Rodin's salutary theoretical realization that the moment can exist only as a series of moments could not, of course, attain any practical reality. Despite Rodin's unselfaware effort to valorize his own work over that of photographers, his sculptures froze a static moment no more and no less than did photographs—just differently. The aspiration to find a representational form that would stitch moments into movement would be answered only yet precisely by the cinema. The aesthetics of Cubism, however, responded to the challenge of photography by articulating a third representational possibility that would neither, as in Lessing, isolate itself to one discrete moment nor, as in Rodin, imagine that one moment could encompass more than one moment. Cubism endeavored to resolve the paradox of the momentary by crystallizing multiple perspectives into one privileged moment. The Cubist artwork's multiple perspectives would reflect the fragmentary nature of modern perception, a connection apotheosized in the widely disseminated images of Picasso's *Demoiselles d'Avignon*.[8]

Yet as Picasso himself indicated, the fixed image of the Cubist artwork could not remain static. "All I have ever made," Picasso said in 1923, "was made for the present and with the hope that it will always remain in the present."[9] This statement strategically conflated two senses of the "present." Picasso valorized the connection between his Cubist style and the dissociated perspectives and perceptions that characterized the modern environment. Like Impressionism before it, Cubism aspired to find a new aesthetic to reflect new modes of sensation and perception in a new social order. This aesthetic in turn expressed the problem of the "present" as an ephemeral, sensual, and momentary category. Picasso's statement yoked together the present moment as a perceptual and discursive form and the present moment of the social reality of modernity. The Cubist impetus arose from the urge to tie these presents together, to express the fragmentation of modern perception as the distension and combination of simple single presents.

This overlapping of moments on the Cubist canvas could be figured as either a temporal or a perceptual structure. The Cubist artist, in André Salmon's conception, must view the object "from all sides at once."[10] The Cubist artwork, in the almost identical terms of Albert Gleizes and Jean Metzinger's 1912 manifesto, demonstrates the "moving around an object to seize several subjective appearances, which, fused in a single image, reconstitute it in time."[11] The canvas provides a blank slate on which to articulate a fixed moment. But the innovation of Cubist aesthetics was to put that moment forward as explicitly constructed and artificial. The moment did not aspire to the imaginary stasis of a photograph or a Rodin sculpture. Rather, the Cubist work openly exploited the destabilizing of a self-present moment and the fragmentation of perception by finding an aesthetic form that would re-present those conditions. This form would articulate a privileged moment that could acknowledge the impossibility of a privileged moment.

For Guillaume Apollinaire in Cubism's third principal manifesto, the Cubist work endeavored "to encompass in one glance the past, the present, and the future." This temporal compression mirrored a spatial condensation in which the work "represents the immensity of space eternalizing itself in all directions at any given moment." Through these double compressions, wrote Apollinaire in a formulation that anticipated André Breton's later conception of the ecstatic Surrealist moment, the "canvas should present that essential unity which alone can elicit ecstasy." [12] Bringing together expansive time, expansive space, and fragmented perception into one crystallized image, the Cubist work could thereby open itself up to the vagaries of future spectatorship: "A picture," said Picasso in 1935, "lives a life like a living creature, undergoing the changes imposed on us by our life from day to day. This is natural enough, as the picture lives only through the man who is looking at it." [13]

The Cubist artwork would be both fixed and fluctuating; it relied on the tradition of the privileged moment while appropriating that concept for a new awareness that that moment could stay still neither through time nor as time, neither in the moment of perception nor in the moment of reception. The Cubist momentary became paradoxical, strategic, and ironic, undermining the validity of a fixed present moment from within painting's inescapable form: a fixed present moment. In this way, Cubist aesthetics aspired to reconcile the parameters of the static canvas to the perceptual, temporal, and spatial transformations of modernity. The Cubist moment went as far as it could go inside the fixed canvas toward finding a form to express modernity's distended moment, an effort indebted to photography and Impressionism while the logical next step of both.

• • •

I'm not much of a gambler, but Breton likes to play the horses, and I've been hanging out with him at the track, watching the horses.

When you look at them hurling themselves around the oval, there do

seem to be times when they're floating in the air, as if they move ahead
by pitching themselves forward and leaping from ground to ground.
As if horses were part of the evolutionary line that includes kangaroos.
Are they?

· · ·

But let's say a horse really does lift all its legs off the ground—how would
we know it, how could we see it, how could we get that moment back
to prove it?
This could make you crazy, trying to get that moment back, trying to
seize it and freeze it and say: look, can't you see it's there?
But you could never be sure; you could never confirm it.
Of course, Columbus and Galileo and Einstein and Wegener and Darwin
could never prove it either.
But don't tell that to Leland Stanford.
If you've got enough money to start a university, you've got enough money
to try to grab that lost moment.
Stanford hired a photographer to show that a horse would at some point
hike all its legs up off the ground.
Think about the obsessiveness of this.
Think about being so possessed by finding and owning that lost moment
that you'll hire a man to spend five years figuring out how to do it.

· · ·

In 1872 Stanford hired a photographer named Eadweard Muybridge, who
eventually figured out how to set up trip wires to snap the horse's movement as a series of frozen moments, one after another after another
after another, to identify and memorialize that moment when all four
of the horse's legs levitated off the ground.
To make a long story short, he proved it.
Now what?
Catching Stanford's mania like flu, Muybridge spent the rest of his life
breaking everything down into serial moments.

Women, men, animals—he didn't care, so long as he could put each moment on the page, sternly surrounded by a black frame as if forcibly to restrain it from spilling into the next moment.

• • •

At more or less the same time in France, Etienne-Jules Marey got the same idea and inflicted it on birds.

He held up a gun, and just when the bird thought the jig was up, it turned out that he was only fooling, that he was using the gun to take pictures.

He called it a chronophotographic gun.

It snapped off shots of one moment after another after another of the bird's flight.

He took those moments and pasted them next to one another in a collage of movement. Movement as collage.

What did this prove?

• • •

OK, unfair question.

Marey and Muybridge wanted to show us that movement is movements, that it's not continuous though it seems to be, that it's always a series of moments.

Is movement continuous? Marey and Muybridge say yes.

Is movement fragmentary? Marey and Muybridge again say yes.

They couldn't figure out what they wanted to say, what their data concluded.

Movement is actually fragmentary; fragments really move.

But which is it?

• • •

What I mean to say is Marey and Muybridge were both acting as advance men for the presence of the present.

They explored fragmentation, but they didn't mean it.

They were acting in bad faith, as double agents for the present.

Putting those hard black lines around each moment of presence, Muybridge fetishized it, memorialized it, built a shrine to each lost instant of presence that would otherwise have been pointlessly lost.

This could lead you to madness—trying to go back and find and freeze every lost moment. You won't ever do it.

Muybridge invites us to believe that the loss of each present moment isn't so bad, isn't so final, we don't have to take it so hard. See, there it is, he says, like a father soothing a frightened child. Photography will retrieve it for you.

And Marey, while he's showing how movement is always already a series of fragments, encourages us to think: yes, he's done it, that's what movement is—a collage of fragments and the spaces between them, which just looks like movement.

But which cancels itself out by making the movement self-present—readable, graspable—all over again.

• • •

A continuous movement—composed of moments—is no more or less present and stable than the one moment by itself.

It doesn't matter how many of those moments you paste together on a photo plate, you're not going to pin it down more than if you had just one.

No more or less than the one moment when you stub your toe or squint at the sun or hit the baseball, what we think of as movement, what we give the name "movement," has already happened.

It's gone.

There it is behind you.

You already moved.

Keep up.

That's why they call it movement.

• • •

Marey and Muybridge claim to be trying to examine, track down, dissect, demonstrate the nature of movement—and we've taken them at their word.

But really they're propagandists for the existence of movement in the first place.

Their desperate, doomed effort to rake back through those lost moments and recompose the movement presumes in the first place that the movement can be found, read.

Not composed, but re-composed.

Not presented but re-presented.

There is no movement in the first place to be reassembled.

They're piecing back together something that's already a trace, already a re-presentation of what's gone, already secondary.

You can feel how badly they want it.

•   •   •

If there is no present, there can be no re-present.

If nothing matches up with itself, the re-presentation cannot match up with its source either.

There's a tripling of absence: the present is empty; the re-present, itself now a present, is empty; and the joint that connects the re-present to the first present is therefore a compound emptiness.

There's always space left over inside and outside the matching-up of the so-called representation and the so-called original.

There's too much space between them but also too many spaces inside them.

They can never meet; neither the parts nor the wholes can mesh; they're getting further and further apart all the time.

Each act of representation comes to us haunted by its incompletion and hollowness, its inability to close on itself.

Muybridge turns out to be the artist of emptiness, the one who found a form for the re-presentation of vacant space, for the hollow futility of the project of representation.

He shows us that the continuous moments cannot simply follow one another.

He doesn't see that that's the beginning of the end.

• • •

In the wake of Muybridge and Marey, cinema assumed its role as the savior of lost presents.

What a great myth for the twentieth century.

You can have it all.

The movies' great appeal is not simple voyeurism, as so many people assume.

It's the voyeurism of loss.

Staring slack-jawed at loss in motion, corpses on parade.

Cinema offers the illusion of movement and depth and it looks like life and it's cool to see it so big on-screen.

Movies also and quietly offer the illusion of conquering absence, mastering loss, vanquishing death.

Not just because we can see people who're dead, though that's more and more true, but because everything on-screen is by definition dead.

Night of the Living Dead rather than *Rear Window.*

• • •

But movies aren't just or simply about the living dead.

They're about the insertion of the dead into empty space, the making-present of the past inside the hollows opened up in the act of re-presentation.

Trying to exhume lost presents, the necrophiliac act of re-presentation transplants something originally incomplete and fragmentary into a new form that is itself (now doubly) broken-up and hollowed-out.

This is how Muybridge and Marey saw what was going to be cinema.

• • •

The Defamiliarizing Moment

Modern discourses of the moment, beginning in the aesthetics of Walter Pater in the early 1870s, became a central chapter in the history of writing and conceiving pleasure. The moment provided a means to conceive a pleasure so intense that it tapers off as soon as it is first felt. The experience of strong sensation articulates the possibility of a moment both through a fervor of feeling that communicates immediate presence and through the waning of strength by which the moment contrasts with the less intense moment that follows it. This momentary bliss resembles traditional conceptions of the sublime; but beginning with Pater and continuing through such new sublimists as Heidegger and Jean Epstein, the sublime moment was redefined for modernity as fully fleeting and fully physiological, a conception of pleasure that eventually played out in Roland Barthes's poststructuralist theories of pleasure.

Sublime sensation, however, formed only one manifestation of the moment's contextual function. More broadly, the moment possessed the power to shake up drift through its intrinsically defamiliarizing quality. By definition detached from ordinary life, the moment became a vehicle of defamiliarization or, more exactly, defamiliarizing by definition, arising by way of contrast with what surrounded it. The moment's unexpected, shocking quality emblematized the concept of defamiliarization as a moment of sudden insight. "Habitualization," as Victor Shklovsky wrote in his 1917 manifesto, "devours works, clothes, furniture, one's wife, and the fear of war. . . . And art exists that one may recover the sensation of life; it exists to make one feel things, to make the stone stony. The purpose of art is to impart the sensation of things as they are perceived and not as they are known." [14]

An isolated moment provides the ultimate form of defamiliarization, as it frames a peak instant of insight, marked off from drift. But defamiliarization's power lies in its dialectical relation to the familiar; it can occur only as a sudden, rude intrusion into the familiar. The defamiliarizing effect wanes and soon evaporates once the momentary shock of this disruption is felt. By definition, the project of defamiliarization can only be momentary: the defamiliarizing moment arises as sudden contrast, but as soon as it is felt or perceived, it becomes less defamiliarizing.

This power of the defamiliarizing moment was set against the complacency of ordinary life above all by the French Surrealists, who drew on that form of the Freudian moment called the uncanny, in which an eerie manifestation of a repressed phenomenon "returns" inside everyday life. The uncanny describes the moment of fright or shock when a repressed phenomenon recurs in the form of an eerie double.[15] Whether as a literary figure or as a spooky moment in ordinary life, the uncanny relies on discrete iconic moments: "Dismembered limbs, a severed head, a hand cut off at the wrist, feet which dance by themselves—all these have something peculiarly uncanny about them, especially when, as in the last instance, they prove able to move of themselves in addition" (397), Freud poker-facedly wrote. Death-in-life arises in momentary eruptions that transfigure re-presentation into a fuzzy afterimage of the life it reiterates. Freud allied this resurgence to both repetition-compulsion and the fear of losing vision, itself a displacement of the "dread of castration" (383). "That factor," he wrote, "which consists in a recurrence of the same situations, things and events . . . does undoubtedly . . . awaken an uncanny feeling, which recalls that sense of helplessness sometimes experienced in dreams" (389).

Freud's essay weaves a cinematic skein of images around momentary re-presentation; tying vision to death-in-life to re-presentation, he winds up close to a conception of the cinematic momentary as a form of deathly re-presentation. Through emblems of castration, the return-of-the-repressed creates momentary disruptions of the unthinking flow of regular life, reminders of what has been suppressed to allow the normal to seem normal.[16] Self-awareness— moments of defamiliarizing insight—occur under the sign of the uncanny in fleeting, barely perceptible moments whose significance can be construed only after the fact. The uncanny moment in this way translated into the language of psychoanalysis the split between the evanescent moment of initial impact and the secondary operation required to make meaning out of that impact. Freud called that retrospective construction of meaning secondary revision, a concept that figured as an explicitly representational process James's invocation of the "vaguely vanishing backward and forward fringe" that construes the moment beyond its first moments.

For the Surrealists, cinema best demonstrated this disruptive power of a defamiliarizing moment. "Essentially," Antonin Artaud wrote, "the cinema reveals a whole occult life with which it puts us directly into contact."[17] Or, as Germaine Dulac suggested in the 1920s, "The cinema is an eye wide open on life, an eye more powerful than our own and which sees things we cannot see. . . . it teaches us things which, without it, we would not know."[18] This power of momentary in-sight emerged first in photography and was therefore most evident in the close-up, film's nearest element to pure photography. "By close-ups of the things around us," Walter Benjamin put it, "by focusing on hidden details of familiar objects, by exploring commonplace milieus under the ingenious guidance of the camera, the film . . . extends our comprehension of the necessities which rule our lives."[19]

The close-up detaches itself from the rest of the film to draw our attention to one important thing. "No longer representational and simply part of the story," as Richard Abel writes, "they became images with a life of their own."[20] The close-up instantiates not just film's defamiliarizing power but also its most fully developed form of the moment. Marking out an isolated instant and underlining that moment as significant in relation to the rest of the drama, it provides film's closest analogy to the frame around the painting, to the frozen instant memorialized by the photograph. It puts forward a peak of attention, a clarifying instant of insight, a detached moment of defamiliarization.

The most overt form of film's defamiliarizing moment appeared in what Tom Gunning calls the "cinema of attractions" of the period before 1908.[21] The cinema of attractions did not present the viewer with a lengthy linear narrative but with brief images designed to shock, thrill, or incite curiosity—for instance, the 1895 Lumière short of a train arriving at a station or a 1903 Edison short in which an elephant is electrocuted, falls over, and dies. Rather than contrive an elaborate story, the cinema of attractions accosted the viewer with cinema; attractions solicited the viewer's attention not as the narratively absorbed voyeur of later cinema but as the gaping,

45

amazed observer also engaged by the circus and the amusement park. The attraction linked the emerging form of cinema to the momentary culture from which it arose: "The attraction," as Gunning notes, "seems limited to a sudden burst of presence . . . to the pure present tense of its appearance."[22]

These attractions were often shown as part of a longer program of skits or short films; their momentary nature was subsumed into their place in a continuous entertainment. This interaction between the momentary and the continuous set the terms for the development of cinema, as the incorporation of moments of attraction into the continuity of full-length cinema mirrored the inculcation of momentary experience into the general continuity of movement and experience. This disruption of a film's putative continuity by moments of attraction was first identified in 1923 by Sergei Eisenstein, who wrote that what he called attraction in theater "is every aggressive moment in it, i.e., every element of it that brings to light in the spectator those senses or that psychology that influence his experience—every element that can be verified and mathematically calculated to produce certain emotional shocks in a proper order within the totality."[23] As Jacques Aumont has written, Eisenstein derived this concept of the attraction from the kinetic spectacles of modernity: "The attraction," Aumont indicates, "is originally the music hall number or sketch, a peak moment in the show, relatively autonomous, and calling upon techniques of representation which are not those of dramatic illusion, drawing upon more aggressive forms of the performing arts (the circus, the music hall, the sideshow)."[24] Marked off from what surrounds it, the attraction represents a momentary apex of attention or stimulation; it offers a mode of experience different from the dramatic storytelling that enmeshes it.

• • •

In a lot of families—I know it's been true in mine—there's one kid who winds up taking care of the parents when they get old. You know what it's like. Everyone else grows up, gets jobs, moves away. One child stays in town, stays in the house, takes control of the parents' lives. That child starts to think she or he knows best. Everyone starts feeling resentful.

Marey and Muybridge are like old parents waiting for the one child to stay home and take care of them.

As if by multiplying the moments, by having more and more and more of them, they can stop them from going away.

Maybe just one, maybe just you, don't you want to stay another minute?

All the others are leaving me. Won't you stay a minute?

Will you also betray me?

Surely one of you will come take care of me here.

As if by throwing all these moments at us, we won't notice that multiplying the problem won't solve it or change it or make it go away.

• • •

Walter Benjamin: The Moment of Shock

The notion that modernity resided in a cinematic immersion in momentary experience was above all exemplified in the intricate analyses of Walter Benjamin, especially the *Passagen-Werk,* or Arcades Project, his compendium of epigraphic reflections on the late-nineteenth-century Paris shopping arcades and the new culture of modernity that surrounded them. Writing in Berlin in the 1930s, Benjamin sought to understand the culture of urban modernity that had emerged in the two previous decades by way of the culture of late-nineteenth-century Paris that gave rise to that modern environment. "For the materialist historian," as he observed in the *Passagen-Werk,* "every epoch with which he occupies himself is only a fore-history of the one that really concerns him."[25] This three-way set of historical Chinese boxes allowed Benjamin's highly compressed meditations to synthesize most of the conceptual and experiential elements that defined modern experience into the 1920s. From his perspective in the Berlin of the 1930s, Benjamin occupied a position inside the modern climate he analyzed yet distanced enough to become retrospectively analytic. Looking back at the emergence of the modern environment, Benjamin found in late-nineteenth-century Paris the blueprint for the developing conditions of modern experience.

Benjamin came increasingly to define modern experience as the

47

flashing, fleeting experience he associated with the moment of shock. If modern life, as Benjamin wrote in his essay on Baudelaire, initiated "a change in the structure of . . . experience,"[26] this change lay in the direction of the momentary and the fragmentary, qualities that for Benjamin transformed the nature and experience of art, history, and time. This vision of the experience of modernity devolved around the contrast between the continuous and the momentary, which he described as "a flash of lightning." The rise of urban modernity replaced experience as a continuous cumulation with experience as momentary shocks that bombard and shatter subjective experience like hand grenades. Baudelaire, Benjamin suggested, "placed the shock experience at the very center of his artistic work" and as a result "indicated the price for which the sensation of the modern age may be had: the disintegration of the aura in the experience of shock."[27]

The continuity of experience has been forever ruptured by the momentariness of modern experience; shock creates a moment, and that moment's intensity prevents time from being either continuous or homogeneous. The intensity of feeling that defines shock placed emphatic brackets around the heightened moment in which the shock is felt. If our lives consist of a series of moments that pass away before we can recognize and acknowledge them, the moment of shock returns to our sensation and perception, and after these to our consciousness, the immediacy of the present moment even as it inexorably slips away. Shock jolts the modern subject into tangible reawareness of the presence of the present.

Benjamin evolved these themes throughout his work, but they came to fullest fruition in the so-called *Passagen-Werk* left unfinished at his death. This project, as described by translator Richard Sieburth, was

> composed of hundreds of 22×28 centimeter sheets of yellowish paper that have been folded in half to create 14×22 folios, the first and third sides of which contain Benjamin's miniscule notes in blue or black ink. Each group of these folios is in turn gathered into a *Konvolut* or sheaf according to its central paradigm or theme. The manuscript is divided into 36 such sheafs, their titles keyed to the letters of the alphabet.[28]

As this description implies, the form of the Arcades Project was fragmented and fragmentary. It proceeded not as a linear argument but as a series of discrete ideas, observations, and quotations, presented without transitions or commentary. Benjamin, Sieburth suggests, "was definitively moving beyond the essay form into the fragmentary tractatus à la Schlegel, Novalis, Nietzsche or Wittgenstein" (41). "Indeed," he elsewhere indicated, "it may be a misnomer to speak of it as a *work* at all . . . Benjamin, by contrast, describes his Arcade not as a work but as an ongoing event, a peripatetic meditation or *flânerie* in which everything chanced upon en route becomes a potential direction his thoughts might take."[29]

Benjamin allied this conceptual collage to the montage of cinema. "This project . . . is intimately linked to that of montage," he stated, elaborating a few sections later: "Method of this project: literary montage. I need say nothing. Only exhibit."[30] More important, the project aimed "to carry the montage principle over into history." Benjamin strove not just to propose the momentary as a defining trope of the modern but to illustrate it through his sensibility and style. In this effort, he refused to distinguish between quotations and commentary; quotations became not marginally illustrative but the core of the project. As Sieburth reports, "Of the quarter of a million words that comprise Tiedemann's edition, at least 75 percent are direct transcriptions of texts Benjamin collected over thirteen years" (28).

This jostling of otherness, panoply of voices, and disjunction of ideas and styles stylistically reflected Benjamin's sense of modernity as filled with anarchic juxtapositions, random encounters, multiple sensations, and uncontrollable meanings. The experience of wandering through the Arcades Project would resemble as closely as possible the lost experience of wandering through the arcades. The arcades would be not just exhumed but reevoked, reexperienced. Benjamin's effort to derive a fragmentary style reflected his insistence that the nature of perception in modernity was intrinsically fragmentary and that a critical record of those perceptions could therefore not imbue them with a false and inappropriate continuity. Hannah Arendt identified the importance of this fragmentary method for Benjamin in her 1968 introduction to the *Illuminations* collection:

49

When he was working on his study of German tragedy, he boasted of a collection of "over 600 quotations very systematically and clearly arranged" . . . ; like the later notebooks, this collection was not an accumulation of excerpts intended to facilitate the writing of the study but constituted the main work, with the writing as something secondary. The main work consisted in tearing fragments out of their context and arranging them afresh in such a way that they illustrated one another and were able to prove their *raison d'être* in a free-floating state, as it were. It definitely was a sort of surrealistic montage.[31]

Benjamin's work suggested, in other words, the interdependence between the category of the moment and the category of the fragment. As a way to express the prevalence of the moment in modern experience, Benjamin took recourse in a fragmentary method. The writing of history will reflect the blunt juxtaposition of fragments that Benjamin associated with montage; the history and criticism of the fleeting, fragmentary shocks of modernity will be fleeting, fragmentary, and shocking. And Benjamin was not just prescribing that history but writing it. "The first stop. . . ," he indicated in the *Passagen-Werk,* "will be to carry the montage principle over into history" (51).

This approach to writing history stemmed from a broader reconceptualization of the experience of time and therefore of time as history and history as time. For Benjamin, the reiteration of the past could occur only as a fleeting moment. "The past," he suggests, "can be seized only as an image which flashes up at the instant when it can be recognized and is never seen again."[32] In the Arcades Project, this sense of the present moment as a "flash of lightning" became Benjamin's governing view not just of time but also of history.

It isn't that the past casts its light on what is present or that what is present casts its light on what is past; rather, an image is that in which the Then and the Now come together into a constellation like a flash of lightning. In other words: an image is dialectics at a standstill. For while the relation of the present to the past is a purely temporal, continuous one, the relation of the Then to the Now is dialectical: not of a temporal, but of an imagistic nature. (50)

In this compressed formulation of the momentary present, Benjamin, like Heidegger, linked the possibility of presence to vision, to what he called throughout the Arcades Project the "Now of recognizability."[33] The possibility of a "Now" can arise only in its tangible—that is, visual—"recognizability." "The dialectical image is a lightning flash. The Then must be held fast as it flashes its lightning image in the Now of recognizability. The rescue that is thus—and only thus—effected, can only take place for that which, in the next moment, is already irretrievably lost" (64).

These three sentences crystallize Benjamin's conception of the momentary. The moment of presence, the Now, occurs as a hiatus in the otherwise ceaseless cyclicity of the dialectic, which circles between future and past. Benjamin later clarified this idea: "Thinking involves both thoughts in motion and thoughts at rest. When thinking reaches a standstill in a constellation saturated with tensions, the dialectical image appears. This image is the caesura in the movement of thought." The possibility of a moment happens in the form of an image, because the perception of an image represented for Benjamin the best option for tangible awareness. This image is what Benjamin called the "Now of recognizability": the Now can occur only in recognizability, and recognizability in turn inscribes the possibility of an instantaneous Now "blasted out of the continuum of the historical process" (67).

But even this tentative and unstable present is immediately rendered a futile "rescue" since its frozen image "in the next moment, is already irretrievably lost." The dialectical image cannot halt the inevitability of the moment's erasure by the next moment, the unstoppability of serial moments. For Benjamin, this procession of discrete, serial moments goes by the name "history." As Sieburth puts it:

"Epic history" in the same sense as Brecht's "epic theater," the Arcades Project will not only administer the shock therapy of montage . . . but more importantly, by deploying its materials into a rhythm of caesurae it will break the illusion that anything like continuity or causality connects past to present. . . . history is not a cumulative, additive narrative in which the uninterrupted syntagm of time flows homogeneously from past to future, but rather a montage where any moment may enter into sudden adjacency with another. History as parataxis — time scattered through space like stars, its course no longer taking the form of progress but leaping forth in the momentary flashes of dialectical constellations.[34]

In Benjamin's terms, modernity articulates a widespread, interlocking system of fragments and moments reaffirmed in time, in vision, and in the structure of history that governs our understanding of past, present, and future. This fragmentation of modern life communicated itself in the experience of the urban street, traversed by vision, motion, and perception. Benjamin's urban subject was bombarded by stimuli and distractions from different directions, barraging and overloading sensation and perception. The transformations of perception that constituted modernity invoked a new kind of discontinuous, momentary attention, attention as distraction, diffused, scattered, and flickering. Benjamin perceived this modern overstimulation as a form of assault against which the subject must protect himself or herself: "The greater the share of the shock factor in particular impressions," he emblematically wrote, "the more constantly consciousness has to be alert as a screen against stimuli."[35]

In this way, Benjamin opened the door for modernity's characteristic form of attention: not an even continuity of experience but a mercurial, variable flow of highs and lows, continuous experience broken up by moments of peak attention or stimulation. Attention-as-vision marked experience as a series of moments. The choice of what to look at defined a discrete moment, whose particularity Benjamin contrasted with the general continuity of experience, or *Erfahrung*.[36] This experience of serial moments occurred against the background of perceptual inhibition, in which, as Jonathan Crary puts it, "a normative observer is conceptualized not only in terms of the objects of attention but also in terms of what is not perceived, of the distractions, fringes, and peripheries that are excluded or shut out of a perceptual field." [37] To stop on the street and focus on one thing aims to frame that one thing as an isolated moment. To experience a sublime rush of sensation that passes as soon as it arrives frames a moment, underlines it, isolates it. The experiences of what Benjamin called shock or what Pater called sublime or what Heidegger called the moment of vision or what Epstein called *photogénie* aspired to remove the moment from the flow and flux of time and, like the frame of the painting, declare: This is the present moment, right here, right now.

• • •

The point is that the copulation (perhaps we had better say, the combination) of two hieroglyphs of the simplest series is to be regarded not as their sum, but as their product, i.e., as a value of another dimension, another degree. . . .

For example: the picture for water and the picture of an eye signifies "to weep"; the picture of an ear near the drawing of a door = "to listen." . . .

But this is—montage!

Yes.

It is exactly what we do in the cinema, combining shots that are depictive, single in meaning, neutral in content—into intellectual contexts and series.

This is a means and method inevitable in any cinematographic exposition.

Sergei Eisenstein, "The Cinematographic Principle and the Ideogram" (1929)

• • •

Think of it this way.

Film is defined by rude, clashing frames and scenes and times and spaces, jostling and juxtaposing.

Film is friction. Every film is a friction film.

And friction creates waste, throws off sparks, generates excess. "There is an absolute waste of mechanical energy available to man when heat is allowed to pass from one body to another."

The wasted space is the viewer's place.

Film spectatorship arises on the ground of the empty moment.

•   •   •

Marey and Muybridge show us something more valuable than the movements they think they're documenting.

They show us presentification.

Husserl said there's no present—except maybe there is, but that's another story, and I've said it already—but only presentification, the making-up of a present, the making-present of an imaginary present, the substitution of a fabricated present for a possible present that is already gone and by definition never knowable.

Marey's and Muybridge's pictures present presentification in action. They think they're scientists, showing us what movement's like. But really they're composing the illusion of presence. They're relying on it, buttressing it, trying their hardest to prove and document it.

They succeed better than they imagined.

They demonstrate that the structure of presence is an empty shell. They find an appropriate, memorable way to visualize it.

This is what presentification looks like.

•   •   •

Look at the thick black lines separating the Muybridge moments.

I can't get them out of my head.

I take them personally.

If we read Muybridge's compositions visually, here is what they tell us: a continuous movement is composed of one moment after another plus the spaces between them.

Visualizing presentification, Muybridge shows us, as evenly and predictably as the moments, the empty spaces that make the moments possible.

•   •   •

Or maybe the point is: trying to re-present continuous movement as a series of moments, Muybridge cannot not include the gaps that intervene between the moments.

It would be like painting a landscape and leaving out the sky.

Whether he intends it or not, he stumbles onto—and palpably visualizes—the fact that (what he presents as) empty spaces matter more than (what he presents as) full spaces.

He thinks he's showing the nature of movement.

He's actually showing the impossibility of self-present movement.

But more poignant than either of those, he's certifying the ongoing self-disintegration of representation.

His pictures eat themselves alive as we watch them.

They substantiate the impossibility of their own existence.

• • •

Stanislavsky: The Moment of Concentration

The possibility that there could be such a thing as a moment—isolated and discrete—arose in response to a modern climate of perceptual overload. This widespread notion that presence in modernity could be forged only through mental and physiological effort appears in as potentially surprising a place as the writings and lectures of acting teacher Konstantin Stanislavsky. For Stanislavsky, the actor's task analogized that of the modern subject: the deployment of attention and physiological control to carve focused moments out of the drift and distractions of daily modern life. "What do we see when we examine man's activity in life?" asked Stanislavsky in the Thirties lectures, later collected as *Stanislavsky on the Art of the Stage,* that summed up his ideas about acting in modernity.[38] "What is all his activity composed of?" he continued, still making clear that his interests extended beyond sketching a method of acting. "It is composed of his attention" (141), he answered his own question.

Stanislavsky insisted that attention in modernity could not come easily or naturally, that it must be constructed, concentrated, or, as Max Ernst would put it in a different context, "forced."[39] Attention necessitates effort, which can arise only from the subject's willful control over the body. Stanislavsky's peak moments are not the sublime, intuitive flashes valorized by surrealism but the products of discipline, self-control, and rigorous training. "The moments of instantaneous illumination," he pointedly noted in addressing acting students, "when you suddenly see what has so long been obscure to you, what you have tried so hard to find but could not get to the bottom of, what was so clear to you and yet did not seem to hang together, only come as a result of the concentration of your entire attention" (160). The moment's ephemerality underlines not its unpredictable, intuitive quality but the effort required to create it.

To the extent that Stanislavsky assumed the same emphasis on fluid mobility as other writers in modernity, this environment reaffirmed the importance of moments of rigorous concentration. On the one hand, Stanislavsky celebrated as much as any other writer what he represented as the change and stimulation of modern life. "Everything is in a state of flux," he said. "And if you have stopped even for one instant, you are already lagging behind, and you have already increased the distance between you and your part. . . . Your inner world cannot live on old problems" (238). In this sort of formulation, acting metonymized modern life in general. The effort to forge a moment of concentration on stage responded to the speed of modern life, "which is never at a standstill" (122). "Every life, whatever its shape or form," indicated Stanislavsky, echoing Bergson, "is always movement" (179). Through his technique "intended for living people" (130), Stanislavsky stressed that an actor "cannot be torn out of his life and at the same time be expected to become a real actor" (195). Only through immersion in the tumult of everyday life can the actor bring experience to bear on a role: "You must live your ordinary lives, learning and observing," he told actors. "Your road is the road of developing ever new qualities of sensibility, which come to you as a result of your struggles and victories" (196). The actor's moments on stage become, more than a matter of technique, a repository for the accumulated experience of life. On stage, "I must bring all that ore which I have obtained throughout my life to the surface" (120).

This focusing of experience can occur only through the control of individual moments that Stanislavsky visualized as an on-stage "circle of attention." As a response to distraction, Stanislavsky posed the possibility of physiological and cognitive immersion in a present moment. His theory was subtended by the question, "How can you . . . so harden yourself that the smallest jolts from outside, the smallest shocks and interruptions in rhythm which constantly take place around you . . . do not upset the rhythm and harmony of your own organism?" (144). Although the actor amasses material from daily life, the on-stage circle of attention creates privileged moments divorced from that life. "Remember," he cautioned his students, "that only this particular circle interests you; the rest of the world . . . [does] not exist for you in this 'now'" (167). The image of the circle stressed its function of enclosure. The creative circle, he said, "is that degree of concentration on one single thought in which all the nerves through which attention carries on its work are brought into focus. . . . your attention . . . must also . . . prevent a single stray thought not belonging to the circle by your concentration from interfering with your particular problems" (145, 177). The circle of moments provides a barrier against the distractions and anxieties that surround the modern subject. And the actor must then remain vigilant against distraction at every moment of the performance: "If an actor cannot focus his thought-feeling-word with the utmost alertness and if he does not know how to make all the powers of his organism act in one direction, he is like a flickering light that hurts your eyes. . . . [he] has not only broken his circle, dissociated himself from his part, and distracted his attention, but also gone back to the preoccupations of his private life, and will never be able to enter afresh into the life of his hero" (178–79).

Stanislavsky's peak moment occurs, then, not as a flash of blinding sublime insight but as a result of such elements of physiological discipline as breathing, gesture, and focus on discrete objects and words. Through these devices, the on-stage peak moment becomes an instant of "fusion" in which the actor meshes with the role and this actor/character in turn merges with the spectator. The "actor can begin to create only after achieving complete self-possession and repose" (126), but those moments of self-control emerge only from focused attention and physiological discipline. "It is his attention an actor must do his best to develop and control" (142), Stanislavsky indicated, but control of attention can occur only through the actor's command of breathing, which for Stanislavsky represented the center of physiological activity: for the actor, "his attention and his respiration . . . must be placed by him under control, and . . . he must learn to manage them as centres of the utmost importance" (143). The "first lessons in breathing," he said, "must become the foundation of the development of that introspective attention, on which all the work in the art of the stage must be built" (117).

This physiological attention extended not just to breathing but also to all the body's muscular activity.

> From the very outset, the student-actor must be taught how to concentrate all his attention upon himself, on certain contracted muscles in his body, and how to relax them at will and switch over his entire attention on another definite group of muscles. Such work cannot be boring. It is most interesting work, and in the course of it the student-actor makes the most surprising discoveries every day. (137)

Physiological mastery allows acting to be defined as intense concentration poured into individual moments. "All my system," he said, "amounts to this: to understand the organic moments in your part and to be able to group them logically, reflecting them in a series of truthful physical actions" (160). The performance of a role manifests the same interplay between momentary intensity and inexorable continuity familiar from other discourses of modernity. To constitute this artificially concentrated moment, the actor may employ not simply breathing but also discrete objects or words that compose nodes of focus and thereby advance that vital three-way moment of "fusion" among actor, role, and spectator. "The thought must be fixed entirely and absolutely on one object or idea, and only on it, without breaking the circle of creative attention for anything else" (166). Concentration becomes both function and meaning of the peak moment: "Now we have found the full definition of concentration: a thought enclosed in the creative circle of attention and fixed entirely on a definite point by will and choice will be concentration" (166).

The same purpose can be served by emphasizing either a momentary gesture or an individual word. "The attention of the public . . . is always attracted by gesture," Stanislavsky indicated. Gesture externalizes the physiological concentration that Stanislavsky advocated. "As soon as your entire attention is concentrated on the tips of your toes, you find it easy to manipulate them" (156), he exhorted his actors. This movement makes explicit to the audience that they are being shown a peak moment, a concentrated instant of heightened significance or energy. Stanislavsky called this moment "a fiery ball," an image that captured at once the peak instant's fleeting nature, circular shape, tendency to attract attention, and configuration from strands of differing elements. He made this same point in relation to emphasizing certain words: "The emphatic word is the centre of attraction. In it the whole meaning of the sentence is hidden, and as a result of the combination of attention, strength of the voice, and the amount of feeling put into it, the feeling-thought-word the actor expresses is capable, like a spark, of kindling the enthusiasm of a crowd" (158).

Like the gesture, the word emblematizes the moment's ability to crystallize elements into one dense configuration. Since neither actor nor audience can manifest peak attention at all moments, gestures and stressed words cue the audience to the desired crests of concentration. These moments provide a means for the actor to effect the "complete fusion of the stage and the auditorium" (119) desired in the Stanislavsky system. If the actor can muster physiology and attention to achieve this immersion, then each present moment of the performance will be alive and vivid. In the ideal Stanislavskian performance, the actor will seem to be a person, living and discovering each moment freshly, as if for the first time. Stanislavsky describes the "complete merging of yourself and the character of your part" (195) as an endeavor of identification: "One must get under the skin of a character so thoroughly that, for instance, Anna Karenina should cease to exist merely as a part that has to be presented on the stage, but instead should become a certain woman-actress who shares the same thoughts and ideas as Anna Karenina" (127).

Stanislavsky thereby suggested that the actor will live the role freshly if he or she views each performance as purely momentary: "Each ephemeral 'now' of a man in a part . . . can gain the interest of the audience only when both the man and his part are no longer preoccupied with the same problems as on the previous day, but when the mood and the meaning, comprehended today, have thrown a new light on the part by new intonations" (230). The actor's performance of a role emblematizes evanescence, even or especially as it is seemingly re-created each day. This concentrated moment then marks the site of a fusion between the actor as a character and the actor as a spectator. Speaking of one of his own performances, Stanislavsky indicated that "Stockmann's and Stanislavsky's body and soul fused organically with one another" (118). He knew how Stockmann should look because he was so melded with his role that "it grew naturally out of the inner man" (118). Because the actor creates this uncanny illusion of presence, "the frontiers of space and time that separate the stage from the auditorium are abolished, and the spectator is forced to believe in you, and weep and suffer as well as rejoice and laugh with you" (194–95). At an extreme, the actor's efforts of attention and concentration allow actor and audience to feel as if they are experiencing the same peak inside the same moment, as if they can meld their mutual attention and energy into a shared moment.

The use of discrete moments to structure the chaotic drift of everyday life also became the model of language articulated around 1911 by Ferdinand de Saussure. For Saussure, language could reflect flux and mutability while striving to stabilize them. "Without language," Saussure suggested, "thought is a vague, uncharted nebula. . . . our thought—apart from its expression in words— is only a shapeless and indistinct mass."[40] Language provides momentary constellations that fix flux, yet it also falls prey to changes occasioned by the passage of time. Each word forms a momentary hedge against drift in three ways: it stands apart from the flow of experience, it forms a momentary configuration of signifier and signified, and it brings together sound and thought. In the first place, Saussure insisted that the "linguistic entity is not accurately defined until it is delimited, i.e. separated from everything that surrounds it on the phonic chain. These delimited entities or units stand in opposition to each other in the mechanism of language" (103). Like a snapshot, each word must mark itself off from each word, and it is only these separations that give each word meaning. "In language, as in any semiological system, whatever distinguishes one sign from another constitutes it" (121).

In the contemporary appropriation of Saussure by Jacques Derrida, this principle has become familiar as the idea that, in Saussure's words, "in language there are only differences without positive terms" (120). This emphasis on difference and separation, however productive it has been for Derrida, provides only a partial reading of Saussure, who also emphasized how each word-unit would be individually constituted. We comprehend each word-unit negatively—in its differences from other word-units—but also positively, because the word-unit must be composed of something in order to differ at all. The word is defined not simply by its difference from other words but also as a momentary constellation of signifier and signified. "The linguistic entity," Saussure insisted, "exists only through the associating of the signifier with the signified. Whenever only one element is retained, the entity vanishes; instead of a concrete object we are faced with a mere abstraction" (102–3). The combination of signifier and signified, which would otherwise remain abstract, becomes an "entity," a "concrete object." Their fusion goes by the name "meaning." If meaning is created by the differences between units, that principle relies in the first place on the creation of those discrete units by momentary fusion.

The combination of signifier and signified, however, only expresses the word-unit's more significant union of sound and thought into an indivisible moment called a word. "Language," Saussure suggested, "can also be compared with a sheet of paper: thought is the front and the sound the back; one cannot cut the front without cutting the back at the same time . . . the division could be accomplished only abstractedly, and the result would be either pure psychology or pure phonology" (113). Linguistic meaning arises only from this partnership with sound: "Considered independently, concepts like 'house,' 'white,' 'see,' etc. belong to psychology. They become linguistic entities only when associated with sound-images" (103).

In these conceptions, Saussure articulated in the realm of language the same complex formulations of the moment expressed in other discourses of modernity. The rethinking of words as compounds of sound/thought and signifier/signified reaffirmed yet undermined the possibility of a discrete moment. Each utterance of the word cannot be separated from its constellation of sound and image; yet those references to sound and image inexorably spill toward the future. This is the point made through Saussure by Derrida: "meaning" never actually occurs, as the moment that might produce it is remorselessly pushed into the future by the same mechanics that generate it. The momentary fusion of signifier and signified opens up the only possibility of meaning, but that possibility can never occur in the moment. As Derrida put it, "The first consequence to be drawn from [Saussure] is that the signified concept is never present in and of itself, in a sufficient present that would refer only to itself."[41] Meaning can be generated only by referring outside the moment of meaning, to elements that can themselves accrue meaning only by reference to other elements. Presence can exist solely on the basis of a domino effect that ceaselessly defers the possibility of presence. In this Derridean appropriation of Saussure, presence can never happen at all: each present moment that has ever happened is still spinning through the maze of deferral, getting thinner as it goes, in what M. H. Abrams vividly characterized as "a ceaseless echolalia, a vertical and lateral reverberation from sign to sign of ghostly non-presences . . . bombinating in a void."[42]

In this way, the present becomes by definition the re-present. There are two presents: a putatively present perception that we can only feel, and a concept called "the present" that struggles to make that present re-present. As Husserl indicated, this effort is not just futile but more and more futile with each new passing moment. Anything that might resemble the "present" toward which cognition and discourse aspire is vanishing further and further into the past—even as perception and cognition continue to be swamped with multitudes of new sensations. In the moment arises the notion of groundless repetition, of re-presentations shorn of an originary present. It is not that we cannot conceive re-presentation because the present can no longer exist; rather, we can conceive nothing but re-presentations. We can no longer sustain any distinction between presence and re-presentation, because presence is always already a re-presentation of a vanished presence. The present and the re-present are the same thing.

• • •

If identity can never catch up with itself, it's also always covering its own tracks, backing up on itself, sputtering and backfiring.

It's not as easy as saying that identity is always a re-presentation, always a construction after the fact, because this idea simply rephrases the same linearity, the same self-presence.

Accepting identity as a self-present reconstruction is no different from believing it to be self-present in the first place.

It still moves straightforwardly forward, one pace off.

If you're living in the empty moment, identity doesn't catch up with itself because it's always effacing itself, backing up over its own path.

Identity snarls in the mesh of the empty moment.

The past cannot function as a straight line plowing forward, carrying presence and identity along for the ride.

It can be present only as a re-presentation.

That's a start, not an end.

• • •

Identity emerges as a desperate effort to reconnect the dots of what's inalterably past, gone.

Identity/presence comes forward as a procession of always-already-absent moments.

As a tenuous, insubstantial substance.

As a cover for cataclysmic absence, loss, irretrievability.

As a film.

• • •

Identity/history/presence on the terms of the empty present covers itself
up as it reveals itself.

It would be circular if it were a simple shape at all.

But this kind of identity can arise only in the spaces around shapes, only
in what appears to be left over, left out, left behind.

It's not strictly negative, not strictly empty, neither strictly revealing nor
strictly concealing.

All these options subscribe to a logic of strict presence.

And you have to stop thinking that way.

• • •

How would identity look if it ceased to be simply present?

No, that's not what I mean.

How would identity look if it ceased to appear to be simply present?

If it gave up making polite visits to the scene of presence.

Abandoned that show of clarity, linearity, knowledge.

You can't imagine it, can you.

• • •

In the empty moment, what you call identity ceases to be continuous,
linear, apparent.

It's hazy and insubstantial, a jumbled, fragmented surface.

It skips around from one time to another, from one place to another.

It refuses to respect the need to keep one moment consistent and continuous with the ones that precede or follow it.

It's a film.

• • •

Film.

Oxford English Dictionary.

Old English *filmen*, membrane, caul, prepuce.

Cognate with OFris. *filmene*, skin.

A membrane, animal or vegetable.

An extremely thin pellicle or lamina of any material.

Often applied to the emanations from the surface of bodies . . . which in the philosophy of Epicurus were supposed to be the objects of perception.

A thin pellicle forming a coating or overlying layer.

A thin pellicle or coating of collodion, gelatin, etc. spread on photographic paper or plates, or used by itself instead of a plate.

A slight veil or covering of haze, mist, or the like.

A morbid growth upon the eye.

Also said of the growing dimness in the eyes of a dying person.

Sometimes film of death.

• • •

T H R E E

Peaks and Valleys

In the spring of 1873, the Museum of Copies, which, as its name indicates, devoted its attention not to fetishized high-art monuments but to copies of them, opened in Paris. As Henri Delaborde reported in the *Revue des deux mondes:*

> Several of the copies have an individual accent in the transmission of the ideas of others, a character of relative invention or, if you will, of penetration. . . . Give several skillful painters the same scene to copy: . . . each copy will resemble the model that it must reproduce, and yet these copies will not resemble each other, because those who did them will have been, according to their tastes and their skills, differently moved or preoccupied by the beauties that they had before their eyes.[1]

In the late-nineteenth-century culture of re-presentation, copies could have the personal, idiosyncratic quality of what used to be called originals. Delaborde's logic signaled as potently as did the very existence of a Museum of Copies that a reliance on originary moments was fast expiring. Faith in the truth or value of an original—the need for an original at all—was firmly dissipating.

The interconnections of modernity, cinema, re-presentation, and the momentary can be understood only in relation to this visual culture of late-nineteenth-century Paris from which cinema arose.[2] Beginning from the innovation of photography in 1839 and continuing through the first showings of cinema in 1895, the culture of nineteenth-century Paris not only elaborated the interplay of the momentary and the continuous but also yoked the momentary to re-presentation, visuality, and mobility in the nexus that would eventually give rise to the cinema. This momentary culture, exemplified in the activity of the *flâneur* and predicated on the philosophy of Positivism, manifested itself in a wide range of cultural forms but above all in Impressionist painting, which forged an aesthetic of the momentary out of the paradoxical effort to seize a moment on the terms of its evanescence.[3]

The most overtly precinematic fulcrum of reality, mobility, re-presentation, and the momentary occurred in the "public taste for reality" that Vanessa R. Schwartz has located in a spectrum of new forms for representing reality in late-nineteenth-century Paris, above all the wax museum and the public morgue.[4] Schwartz's analysis of these cultural phenomena suggests the extent to which late-nineteenth-century Paris set the pace for a modern culture in which the lines between reality and representation became increasingly indistinct. The morgue, for example, became a wax museum in reverse when it opened its doors to the public, ostensibly to identify the anonymous dead, and thereby created a free popular entertainment at which families jostled each other to gape at real immobile bodies.

These forms may have literalized re-presentation, but their stasis was predicated on the viewer's mobility. As viewers strolled through the Musée Grévin, Paris's popular wax museum, their movement was interspersed with gawking at static wax forms. Indeed, the Musée Grévin eventually moved beyond fixed statues to present such serial narratives as the "History of a Crime," which portrayed seven scenes of a crime from the initial murder to the murderer's execution. "If spectators' movement might have been incorporated into the museum's display," Schwartz indicates, "narrativity also built motion into the displays" (310). The wax museum presented not simply momentary glimpses of the real-as-representation and not simply a strolling experience that mimed *flânerie* but above all an interplay between the momentary and the continuous. The resurgence in popularity of panoramas and dioramas in this period similarly combined the viewer's mobility with the re-presentation of frozen moments: "The panoramas' realism," Schwartz notes, "hinged on the notion that, to capture life, a display had to reproduce it as bodily, and not merely as visual, experience" (311).

These phenomena resituate the origins of cinema as a result not simply of technological advancements and narrative precursors but of a wider momentary culture of movement, spectatorship, and the re-presentation of reality. This culture stretched from Impressionist painting to baseball, from circuses to Positivist philosophy. And this prehistory of the moment indicates that the textualization of experience, in which the "real" could increasingly be understood only as re-presentation, occurred as a function of the momentary, which was in turn a function of the loss of a present moment and the concomitant emphasis on the bodily and visual experiences of the individual body. This mobilized body, however, was also an unstable body, as ephemeral and mercurial as movement itself. With the mobilization of the body came the parallel yet paradoxical effort to regulate that mobility, to channel attention and structure the subject's potentially anarchic participation. This endeavor, which found its ultimate outlet in the patterned attention of cinema, struggled to structure drift into a workable process as it created the ground on which drift could arise.

• • •

In his 1911 *Principles of Scientific Management,* Frederick Winslow Taylor described his harassment of a Bethlehem Steel worker named Schmidt.

"Schmidt, are you a high-priced man?" Taylor asks and reports Schmidt's logical answer, "Vell, I don't know vat you mean."

"What I want to find out is whether you want to earn $1.85 a day or whether you are satisfied with $1.15, just the same as all those cheap fellows are getting."

"Did I vant $1.85 a day? Vas dot a high-priced man? Vell, yes, I vas a high-priced man."

After more dialogue in this step-by-step vein, Taylor got to the point.

"You know just as well as I do that a high-priced man has to do exactly as he's told from morning till night. . . . [I]f you are a high-priced man, you will do exactly as this man tells you tomorrow, from morning till night. When he tells you to pick up a pig and walk, you pick it up and you walk, and when he tells you to sit down and rest, you sit down. You do that right straight through the day. And what's more, no back talk. Now a high-priced man does just what he's told to do, and no back talk.

"Do you understand that?"

• • •

Taylor also turned his attentions to bicycle-ball inspectors.

"Even when the hours of labor had been shortened from 10½ to 8½ hours, a close observation of the girls showed that after about an hour and one-half of consecutive work they began to get nervous.

"They evidently needed a rest.

"It is wise to stop short of the point at which overstrain begins, so we arranged for them to have a ten minute period for recreation at the end of each hour and one quarter. During these recess periods (two of ten minutes each in the morning and two in the afternoon) they were obliged to stop work and were encouraged to leave their seats and get a complete change of occupation by walking around and talking, etc."

And to bricklayers, reporting on a study by a colleague:

"He made an intensely interesting analysis and study of each movement of the bricklayer, and one after another eliminated all unnecessary movements and substituted fast for slow motions. . . . He developed the exact position which each of the feet of the bricklayer should occupy with relation to the wall, the mortar box, and the pile of bricks."

These procedures achieved Taylor's goals:

"every single act of every workman can be reduced to a science" and

"the substitution of a science for the individual judgment of the workman."

These aims required "a man of the mentally sluggish type . . . so stupid and phlegmatic that he more nearly resembles in his mental make-up the ox than any other type."

. . .

But here's my point.

"The law is that for each given pull or push on the man's arms it is possible for the workman to be under load for only a definite percentage of the day.

"For example, when pig iron is being handled (each pig weighing 92 pounds), a first-class workman can only be under load 43 per cent. of the day.

"He must be entirely free from load during 57 per cent. of the day."

This is the same as Taylor's proposal for the bicycle-ball inspectors.

In Taylor's efficiently dictatorial and dictatorially efficient universe, nothing goes to waste.

Waste is structured into the experience of work and time.

It's wasted yet not wasted.

. . .

This is Taylor's innovation.

He's got a brutal rhetoric, but his thinking turns out to be more paradoxical than it seems.

Let's not try to vanquish waste by wiping it out.

Let's co-opt it, seduce it, bring it into the fold, make it feel wanted and needed.

Waste becomes codependent on work.

It's the underside, the not-work.

Yet it makes work possible.

Work would be nothing without it.

Without waste, work would be like Kelvin's apocalypse of heat, diminishing and diminishing toward final collapse.

Waste snaps work to attention.

Waste defamiliarizes work.

Everything drifts, but it doesn't have to be that way. Structure will save us.

• • •

Peaks and Valleys

"With each crossing of the street," wrote Georg Simmel in his 1903 study "The Metropolis and Mental Life," the city dweller is accosted by "the rapid crowding of changing images, the sharp discontinuity in the grasp of a single glance, and the unexpectedness of onrushing impressions."[5] Simmel's description, itself crowded with perceptions, gives us a vivid sense of the disjunctions, distractions, and discontinuities that were seen to characterize the emerging experience of modern life.[6] For Simmel, the modern metropolis occasioned an "onrushing" tidal wave of sensations and distractions that overwhelmed the subject's perception. The flood of impressions was constantly changing, filled with unexpected conjunctions and sudden disjunctions. The modern subject processed and perceived these sensory data visually; Simmel's description of "changing images" and of "the grasp of a single glance" takes for granted that the experience of the modern city was visual, that vision marked the intersection between the subject's perception and the modern phenomena that surrounded it.

In analyzing this climate, Jonathan Crary has written that attention and distraction in the modern environment "were not two essentially different states but existed on a single continuum. . . . Attention was described as that which prevents our perception from being a chaotic flood of sensations, but research showed it to be an undependable defense against such chaos." As Crary goes on to note, the fixed focus of attention "always contained within itself the conditions for its own disintegration" in the diffuse focus of distraction.[7] Modernity's visual environment plunged the subject into a ceaselessly shifting effort at selection and attention; this process expressed itself in discrete moments through which the urban subject could attempt to fix the panorama of changing impressions. Each "single glance," in Simmel's terms, endeavored to "grasp" as many "changing images" as it could. Yet this effort still failed, since "sharp discontinuity" characterized even these individual frames, and the subject in each successive moment always again fell prey to "the unexpectedness of onrushing impressions."

It is not an accident that Simmel's description of the city could double as a description of the cinema, as the visual, mobile experience of the city set the terms for the eventual emergence, in city culture, of film spectatorship. This new urban experience was embodied in the emblematic figure of the *flâneur,* who strolled city streets on guard for new things to see and sense. As numerous critics have pointed out, the *flâneur* marked the living bodily site on which vision, movement, and sensation precinematically came together. "As a social and textual construct for a mobilized visuality," in Anne Friedberg's words, "*flânerie* can be historically situated as an urban phenomenon linked to, in gradual but direct ways, the new aesthetic of reception found in 'moviegoing.' " [8] More specifically, cinema emerged from the redefinition of spectatorial entertainments not simply as momentary but as a jostling, montagelike structure of peaks and valleys. This momentary culture of modernity manifested itself in a wide range of new cultural forms,[9] all of which can be defined as ventures featuring kinetic, bodily activity; an emphasis on the viewing of moving action; and the demand to focus attention amidst distraction. These activities all relied on attention conceived as momentary and on structure composed from a chain of discrete moments traded off against slack moments. Such entertainments as the three-ring circus, the amusement park, and organized professional sports created the context for the emergence of cinema in their shared identity as modes of mobile, kinetic activity in which the participant's attention was distracted by several things happening at once and structured in peaks and valleys.

The development of the three-ring circus crystallized the new form of attention as visual, mobile, and distracted. The modern circus in the American context began its development in April 1871, when P. T. Barnum joined W. C. Coup and Dan Castello to present a three-acre circus in Brooklyn, the biggest and most consolidated circus yet offered.[10] Coup and Barnum made the shift that brought the circus closer to a modern conception of attention: they added a second ring to their circus, eventually followed by a third. With more than one ring, the circus became an exercise in distraction, as different things going on at the same time competed for the viewer's attention. The circus artists, wrote Morris Werner in his 1923 biography of Barnum, "have considered that their decline in individual popularity was due to the increase in the magnitude of circus presentation, for it was impossible to do stirring or excruciating things . . . when two other groups were occupied in distracting the attention of the audience at the same time."[11]

As Werner indicates, the mobile continuity of the circus performance depended on fixed moments of spectacle. When the circus arrived in Paris at the end of 1901, it was taken as an emblem of the merciless distractions of modern entertainment by such critics as Albert-Emile Sorel, who wrote about the circus in *Revue bleue,* "Attention is never relaxed or stopped on a detail."[12] Sorel's comment captured a characteristic feeling of overstimulation, but he got the circus exactly wrong, because its perceptual activity consists precisely of stopping on serial details. In the face of three rings of chaos, the circus viewer must continually stop on one detail after another; the continuous experience is composed of peaks of spectacle that both succeed and run parallel to one another.

While the circus presented the familiar image of modernity as sensory bombardment, the amusement park moved toward the more fully developed form of modern attention as variable and fluctuating. The amusement park emblematized the leisure activities that arose around the turn of the century for the diversion of working and immigrant urban classes. As Kathy Peiss has noted, these activities included dance halls and nickelodeon parlors, forms of distraction conceived as release and relief from the urban world of work.[13] Amusement parks in such cities as New York and Chicago provided the best diversion, because they afforded literal distance from the city.[14] Yet, ironically, these parks reaffirmed the conditions of modernity as much as they relieved them. Coney Island's Luna Park, in Brooks McNamara's evocative description, "offered visitors a madly eclectic environment which included an Eskimo village, a monkey theatre, a miniature railway, a shoot-the-chutes, and Venetian canals, all illuminated at night by more than 250,000 electric lights."[15] The aura of seaside strolling allowed producers of the Coney Island distractions to draw on the increased appetite for mobile, kinetic sensation while packaging that appeal in the guise of a respite from those sensations.

This distracting atmosphere pointed up the difference between the circus's deployment of a fixed viewer and mobile spectacle and the amusement park's use of a mobile viewer and fixed spectacles. Because the participant was moving, the amusement park created a more fluctuating form of participation. The experience of Coney Island reiterated the peaks-and-valleys structure that governed modern perception in the city, as distractions accosted the subject and forced him or her to focus on some things and screen out others. The amusement park offered a setting of highs and lows in which participants strolled around, joined a thrilling ride, had a snack, strolled around some more. Amusement park–goers, as John Kasson wrote, "could enjoy their own momentary fright and disorientation because they knew it would turn to comic relief."[16] This structure of attention was not just mobile but variable, a form of fluctuating perception institutionalized in the roller coaster, which acted out the highs and lows that characterized the perceptual experience of modernity.[17]

The redefinition of attention into peaks and valleys underlined the sense that modern life was increasingly dominated by moments and fragments rather than by continuity and homogeneity. More to the point, this reconceptualization of attention into peaks and valleys provided a regulated structure whereby forms of entertainment endeavored to control the participant's potential for unpredictably fluctuating attention. The emergence of baseball, football, and basketball in the late nineteenth and early twentieth centuries in the United States demonstrated this reliance on moments of peak attention and stimulation.[18] Baseball, football, and basketball were all characterized by the alternation between lulls and bursts of goal-oriented activity. In precinematic entertainment, no form of distraction as fully defined attention as variable and fluctuating as did these sports. The crack of the baseball against the bat and the drop of the basketball through the hoop epitomized entertainment's increasing reliance on the moment. Scoring—moving forward in the game—was tied to mastery of the moment; the moment was framed by the contrast with the less pivotal activities surrounding it, all of which represented not a singular moment but the continuous motion of running across the court, down the field, or around the bases.

Baseball, in particular, was filled with leisurely lolling suddenly broken by the motions of pitcher, batter, and ball. Outfielders and infielders wait around; the pitcher sizes up the situation, stops, tries to pick a man off first, eventually throws a ball at which the batter might not even swing—these slumps are then broken by louder noise and faster motion. For each of the players, the experience of playing the game is defined by the contrast between drifting inaction and surges of activity. The potential for drift and boredom is at each turn set against the reassertion of action, a structure further expanded by football: as Walter Camp developed the game at Yale in the 1880s, he built into it this peaks-and-valleys structure through "downs" that made football, like baseball, an alternation between purposeful motion and lulls of meandering inactivity.[19]

• • •

Man must work . . . and in this alone lies the meaning and purpose of his
    life, his happiness, his ecstasy. . . . In the same way that one has a crav-
    ing for water in hot weather, I have a craving for work. . . . We must
    work, work. That's why we're so melancholy and take such a gloomy
    view of life, because we know nothing of work. We come of people
    who despised work.
This is from *The Three Sisters,* and you see that Chekhov understood the
    seductive pull of drift.
Life is slipping by, never to return, never, we shall never go to Moscow.
I see that we shall never go.

• • •

People in Chekhov's plays fall into three groups.
The ones who hate drift and condemn idleness:
I've been hanging around here with you, and I'm sick and tired of loafing.

I can't live without work, I don't know what to do with my hands. . . .
Forgive me, but I have never seen such frivolous, such queer, unbusinesslike people as you, my friends. You are told in plain language
that your estate is to be sold, and it's as though you don't understand
it. (Lopakhin in *The Cherry Orchard*)

The ones who try to fight it, who know they should, but find themselves
too weak to resist the tide of drift:

Yes, you really ought to change your life, my dear. You really should—
somehow. (Irina in *The Three Sisters*)

Both of you—he and you—have infected us with your idleness. I was
infatuated with you and have done nothing for a whole month; . . .
wherever you set foot, you and your husband, you bring ruin. (Astrov
in *Uncle Vanya*)

And the ones who love the drift, give in to it, luxuriate in it sensually:

You do nothing, fate simply tosses you from place to place—it's so strange.
(Ranevskaya in *The Cherry Orchard*)

Ranevskaya says to Lopakhin:

But what are we to do? Tell us what to do.

It sounds plaintive.

But it's a challenge.

• • •

In *The Cherry Orchard,* Ranevskaya, passively presiding over the demoli-
tion of her orchard like the three sisters who never muster the energy
to go to Moscow, is meant to represent the old world, lazy and spoiled
and indolent, whereas Lopakhin, industriously buying up and knock-
ing down the orchard, stands for modernity, vigorous and purposeful.

Everything that is now unattainable will some day be comprehensible
and within our grasp, only we must work. . . . The great majority of
the intelligentsia that I know seek nothing, do nothing, and as yet are
incapable of work. . . . all our fine talk is merely to delude ourselves
and others. . . . to begin to live we must first atone for the past, be done

with it, and we can atone for it only by suffering, only by extraordinary, unceasing labor. (Trofimov in *The Cherry Orchard*)

Except it's not that simple.

Ranevskaya grasps drift's langorous allure but also its power and resistance, its force as not simply work's underside but an energy in its own right.

Proust saw this too, and like Madame Ranevskaya he gave in to the drift, immersed himself in it, let it carry him away.

You do nothing, fate simply tosses you from place to place.

It's so strange.

. . .

This is my point.

People think modernity is about the energy, the purpose, the charged moments.

But it's about the drift.

You can't get away from the drift.

You can't resist its pull.

Let it draw you in.

Drift is as close as you get to feeling the empty moment.

It's a first step.

Try it on.

See how you like it.

. . .

Taylor saw the centrality of drift and decided to accommodate it.

He was clever and strategic, like a wily general.

But he had a bad attitude.

He perceived his role as vanquishing drift.

Wanting to increase efficiency and productivity, he thought he could co-opt the enemy rather than give in to it.

What made him believe that experience could be neatly divided.

Work and rest, one traded off against the other.

On or off.

• • •

Taylor makes us face a central question of modernity.

What does it mean to waste time?

· What do the words mean?

Time is wasted by nature and by definition.

Time is always already wasted.

There it goes. It's gone.

• • •

So Taylor had it half right.

He saw that activity could be conceived only as a counterpoint, a defamiliarization, against the background of drift.

But he didn't see that it's all drift, all waste.

Or maybe he did—maybe I'm selling him short—because the desperation of his effort to make something of that time, to squeeze activity, efficiency, productivity out of every minute, may show that he knew deep down that it's all waste.

That it's all gone and pointless.

That we're all going to die.

What difference does it make?

The ball inspector won't die any sooner or any later if she takes one minute more or less on break.

• • •

But Taylor's obsessed with control.

This is the downfall of so many people.

It's all chaos.

It's all arbitrary.

Breton with his astrologer, Taylor with his slide rule.

Give in.

Slip into the empty moment.

You don't need to control everything.

You don't need to control anything.

You can't control anything anyway.

Everything drifts.

• • •

Toward Cinema

The emergence of cinema comprehensively brought together the attributes of modernity's distractions and entertainments: the rise of re-presentation; the body as the center of perception, sensation, attention, and mobility; and the interplay between the momentary and the continuous, figured through peaks and valleys as the structure of motion and attention. To the extent that the viewer's drift operates as a parallel track to the forward movement of the film "itself," narrative cinema evolved around the effort to control, channel, and regulate that mercurial drift so as to bring it as closely as possible in line with the readings that the film wants to promote. This endeavor has its roots in the modern urban climate of diffuse attention in which the beleaguered modern subject needed to marshal physiological, perceptual, and cognitive resources to defeat the forces of distraction that at each moment threatened to divert concentration. The attention demanded by modernity set up a tension between the possibility of distraction and the effort of concentration required to stave off that possibility. Modernity's welter of stimulation made attention more crucial yet less feasible. In maneuvering through hazards and distractions, the modern subject's forward motion was predicated on attention as a linear focus that carved a path through time and space. Attention was in this sense visual: it describes those sensations or events on which we choose to fix our gaze, leaving others on the edge. The choice of what to pay attention to was a choice of what to look at. Everything else got left on the periphery of the visual field, defined as distraction.

In this process, the drifting possibilities of distraction assumed a triple meaning: distraction could describe the nature of modern perception, diffused among a multitude of phenomena; the new entertainments responsible for generating that drift; and the limits or breakdown of that perception, in which attention has become too distracted to focus on its target. For such writers as Walter Benjamin and Siegfried Kracauer, the trope of distraction unified the subject's relation to the technologized urban environment and the technologized forms of entertainment that demanded a new form of spectatorship. These writers of the Frankfurt school, in Patrice Petro's paraphrase, considered "the entire urban panorama —moving from photography to film to the city and the street—in an effort to discern how all aspects of modernity register the historical process in which an absorbed or concentrated gaze has been replaced by a more distracted mode of looking." [20]

Cinema, from this perspective, was a distraction and contributed to distraction, yet it also, as a new technology of attention, tried to defeat distraction by marshaling concentration. The structure of peaks and valleys became a way for new forms of entertainment to regulate the attention of their participants. This effort to control perception arose against the background of the mobility and freedom of attention generated by modernity's distractions. With so many things available for sensation and distraction, the modern city opened a freedom of attention; the multitude of distractions combined with the primacy of motion gave modern attention the potential for variation and change. But the newly mobilized body was also an unpredictable body, and forms of entertainment in this period endeavored to regulate this possibility of fluctuating, idiosyncratic participation by providing lulls and slumps in their own structure. The effort to govern the body transfigured momentary attention into a structured mode of participation. Organizing participation in peaks and valleys acknowledged the possibility of fluctuating attention while striving to regulate and channel that attention.

This impulse to fight drift drew on the interlacing of work and rest associated with the industrial efficiency studies of Frederick Winslow Taylor.[21] Taylor's widely influential system created a structure in which work and drift would be not mutually exclusive but mutually reinforcing. While Taylor's method of industrial efficiency influenced the mode of production in classical Hollywood studios,[22] his conception of weaving together work and rest also affected the structure of classical narrative cinema, which aimed to channel the viewer's potential drift, to regulate the process of the viewer's attention. Taylor's time and motion studies of factory work led him to believe that work could be optimally performed only if alternated with unstructured breaks. Because muscles need rest to regenerate their full capacity, work could become efficient and profitable not by battering as hard as possible against drift but by acknowledging drift as an enabling condition of work itself. Taylor suggested that workers, rather than performing work continuously with diminishing returns, could perform an optimal amount of work, take a break, and then return to utmost capacity.

Along these lines, the technique of cinema memorialized a modern conception of attention that strove to regulate the viewer's drift both indirectly (by controlling the process of attention) and directly, by structuring the narrative into what Raymond Bellour has called "slumps" of attention:

> In all classical films, there are moments of inaction. These are undoubtedly necessary to the action, but we experience them as slumps. . . . As if dull or semi-dull moments are necessary to recuperate, reorder what has just been seen, to unbind, even unconsciously, condensations and displacements; in short, these slumps are necessary in order that the spectator may accomplish for himself a first working through of the "film-work."[23]

Classical cinema, as Bellour describes, aspired to turn everything into work, to marshal even the lulls of drift for the production of order and meaning. As Bellour does not acknowledge, this effort may at any point fail and lead the viewer into drifting tangents. Such critics as Stephen Heath, Barthes, and Kracauer have noted in various ways that a film is filled with waste and therefore ripe for the intervention of drift. There are so many extra frames just to get the viewer to perceive one continuous image, so much light, heat, and dust dissipated in projection. And in those images, there is so much more than we really need: "In film," as Heath puts it, "a host of actions can and do enter while remaining outside of any particular—particularising—notation; film, in other words, allows actions in both a simultaneity . . . and a multiplicity."[24] This waste allows us to drift around in the image and settle on stray details that may, as Barthes suggested, "overwhelm the entirety of my reading."[25] These marginal parts of the image, Kracauer wrote in *Theory of Film,* "are particularly fit to function as an ignition spark. Any such shot may touch off chain reactions in the movie-goer—a flight of associations which no longer revolve around their original source but arise from his agitated inner environment. This movement leads the spectator away from the given image into subjective reveries."[26]

As Barthes, Heath, and Kracauer all indicate, the film image becomes fertile ground for drift. In the face of this potential, classical Hollywood narrative functions as a partial restraining line against drift, into which an individual viewer may at any moment fall and from which that viewer may at any moment return. This order was predicated on the peaks-and-valleys pattern incorporated from modernity's momentary culture, which in the period between 1900 and 1920, above all between 1910 and 1920, became film's defining structure of time and space. A primary formal innovation of the period before 1920 was the development of parallel editing, which enabled a filmmaker to edit between two or three actions going on in different places at roughly the same time.[27] This technique moved films away from the static perspective of theatrical representation and allowed filmmakers to regulate the story's suspenseful unfolding. Parallel editing provided a means to control space and time, both of which were busted up by editing's jagged discontinuities. The parallel form aggressively interwove disparate spaces as a means to fragment, reassemble, and elasticize time.

In this evolution, filmmakers began to move away from short depictions of one action toward film's more durable identity as a mixed bag of fragments stitched together by editing. This process involved both parallel editing and the variations of shot distance introduced into early cinema in this same period.[28] Not only hurtling from place to place through parallel editing but also jerking the viewer's attention from longer shots to medium shots to close-ups to extreme close-ups and back again, film began to take its place as the demon child of the overstimulated modern environment. Variations of shot distance, together with parallel editing, defined the new form of attention demanded by cinema: the link between the structural form of fragmentation and the perceptual and experiential form of attention. Parallel editing gave filmmakers a means to regulate the story's pace and duration, how much time it occupied. The variation of distance in space performed the crucial corollary: the effort to control the viewer's attention. This spectatorial attention was, in the process, defined as fluctuating. The close-up emphatically tells the viewer: this is important. It thereby became yet another form of the moment and, like other forms of the moment in modernity, stood out as significant, as a peak of attention, only in contrast to what surrounded it. This structure of contrast, of peaks and valleys of attention and stimulation, was built into cinema's governing assumptions through the structure of longer shots and closer shots, a structure in which we are meant to read distance as proportional to significance: the further away the camera, the less pivotal the action.

By putting peak moments into motion, film techniques forged the impossibility of presence into a new form of spectatorial participation. Editing created a collage of fragments that could not help but render the viewer's experience discontinuous. This discontinuity opened gaps and spaces throughout the action, nagging echoes of discontinuity that haunt a film's premise of continuity.[29] Film's narrative shape of peaks and valleys emerged from the intersection between film's form as a series of moments and the dramatic structures film borrowed from theater, melodrama, and the nineteenth-century realist novel. These modes relied on climax and exposition, on suspense and release, in ways that mitigated but did not eradicate the film strip's one-thing-after-another technology. Peaks and valleys provided a means to vary the viewer's experience of a film's durational uniformity. This use of peak moments in the climate of modernity permanently shaped film structure in a pattern deployed from the romance's climactic kiss to the horror film's alternation between suspense and slashing attacks to the musical's eruptions of song and dance to the action film's explosions, car crashes, and shoot-outs. In the words of Joel Silver, the prototypical producer of 1980s action films: "The rule of thumb is that in every reel of a movie—that means basically every ten minutes—if you're making an action movie, every ten minutes you must have an action beat. Something dramatic and jolting must happen. . . . People come to the movies we do and they come out having had a roller-coaster ride."[30] Cinema's uneven and unceasing movement aimed to keep modern subjects so busy in mobile, kinaesthetic activity that they would forget or—better yet—never realize that in the absence of presence their perceptual highs and lows could not in fact occur.

FOUR

What's the Use?

       •   •   •

For a long time I used to go to bed early.

That was before I got here.

Now I have no reason to go to bed at all.

I can't get used to it.

I can't write right.

I can't think straight.

Everything's jumpy, disconnected.

It's not my style.

       •   •   •

At first I was glad to be here.

I never liked being dead.

It was boring.

I never liked falling asleep either.

Maybe it was a premonition.

There's nothing to do when you're dead.

Every moment the same as the last, the same as the next.

Trapped in an eternal moment.

Which would be okay if you could be trapped in a great moment.

Imagine being stuck forever in the moment of orgasm.

It doesn't work that way.

· · ·

I learned this about the moment of death.

It's the moment when the body meets itself.

The body catches up to itself at the instant it expires.

Then you're stuck in that moment forever.

That's what it means to be dead.

· · ·

So be glad you didn't die falling off a mountain.

Cold, scared, and lonely.

For the rest of time.

Like Walter Benjamin.

Like people who died in concentration camps.

No one chose it.

It's how it is.

Benjamin saw that it was the same either way.

· · ·

So it's better to be here.

Given the alternatives.

But why can't we get this right?

You've got three choices, and they're all bad.

In life, you can never be in the moment.

In death, you can never get out of the moment.

In the empty moment, you can never stay in the moment.

Well, not never.

It only feels that way.

Sometimes one moment succeeds another.

By accident.

Sometimes a whole series of moments follows one another.

That's bliss.

But you can't count on it.

. . .

I spent my life trying to wander around in bliss.

Trying to keep pleasure going.

To sustain it over as many continuous moments as I could.

I thought if I kept my body in one place, I'd pin pleasure down.

Sitting in bed, I played a game with myself.

I tried to stay inside pleasure for more moments each day.

Stretch it out every day, even if just by one or two seconds.

It was a challenge.

A challenge crossed with hedonism.

My kind of test.

. . .

But here that's pointless.

Sometimes you get moments in sequence.

Sometimes they last a long time.

Hours.

Days.

But you can't count on it.

You never know when it will end.

From one moment to the next, it's over.

You never see it coming.

Continuity becomes a peril, a risk.

That's how they want it.

. . .

The worst part isn't losing the present.

It's losing the hope of the present.

They think I should be grateful to be here.

They think I have an attitude.

They send people to buck me up.

They thought I was living in the past anyway.

But they missed the point.

Roaming around the past was my way to feel the present.

Pulling past into present was a game.

An asymptote.

To see how close I could get without touching.

Now I have nothing.

No present, no past, no future.

No hope.

●　　●　　●

Can you understand how it feels to live in an empty present?

I don't think you can.

In your life, sensation is your best friend.

It deludes you into thinking you can feel a present.

You think: here I am, right now.

You feel it, and you feel it wane.

Maybe you know it can't exist in principle.

There are lots of things that can't happen in theory.

You can still feel them, imagine them.

That's what's called fantasy.

Knowing you can't have someone but envisioning it.

In your mind.

You feel it and you think it and you see it.

Except it's not there.

●　　●　　●

You imagine yourself with another body.

You are in fact with another body.

Technically, conceptually, these have to be the same thing.

You know that everything's a construction.

A representation.

You grasp there's no distinction between imagining and being.

It's all in your mind.

Except they're not the same thing.

We all know it.

But there's no way to explain it, to account for it.

That's how bodies vanquish presence.

•   •   •

I got so enamored of this idea.

I tried to make it work.

It seemed an ingenious solution.

Philosophy put into practice.

In the service of pleasure.

Except it doesn't work.

It's not the same.

I can't say why.

There's no reason why.

It's not in the realm of reason.

You have to accept it outside logic.

Bodies spinning in their own realm.

Something happens there.

We don't know what it is.

We're trying to catch up.

•   •   •

Imagine how much worse the problem is here.

The split between the body and the mind.

I haven't even tried.

Breton and Picasso have.

Picasso can't control himself.

And Breton keeps chasing after that ecstatic moment.

95

He can't live without it.

It's like a drug.

He can't live without the moment of encounter.

Pater has the same problem.

But he sits quietly in the corner changing the channels.

He has some decorum.

Breton's out there every night.

It's futile.

It's never going to happen.

But he doesn't give up.

● ● ●

He has to know that he's never going to feel a moment.

Never.

He needs to get the point and move on.

Presence is a drug.

You still want to feel it.

You still need to feel it.

You can't live without it.

That's why, being without it, you can't be strictly living.

● ● ●

In your life you can't feel a moment either.

But you think you can.

That's the difference.

You've got your illusions.

You can live with them.

They allow you to keep going.

You know there's no present.

It makes no practical difference.

You go through your life.

You don't feel like you're not present.

You don't think about it.

Your body and mind cooperate to let you forget it.

• • •

Here you can never forget it.

Here you can't think about anything else.

Here you're confronted at every moment by what you've lost.

Here you know there's no present.

And you can't feel it either.

You can't fool yourself.

Not for one moment.

Imagine living like that forever.

• • •

But let's say you can get around that.

I'm not saying you can.

I couldn't say myself.

But let's stipulate that you can.

You still have to face the discontinuity.

One moment won't necessarily follow another.

Think about it.

You're with someone.

You're getting somewhere.

And then you're in the sixteenth century.

Seduction presumes linearity.

A buildup, a teleology.

One thing leads to another, as they say.

No linear time, no journey of enticement.

This must be why Breton fights so hard to get it back.

• • •

I spent a lot of time on this problem.

Thinking I could have someone in my mind.

I'm an imaginative fellow, sensual, creative.

I could have whoever I wanted.

And I could control it.

It would be not just the same as having the person.

But better.

Without the problems of a real person.

All the ways things can go wrong.

Get messy.

Disappoint.

Fail.

•　•　•

So do you wonder why I never leave my room

What's the use?

I won't say I'd rather be dead.

But it's not much of an alternative.

Some people love the uncertainty.

The danger.

The spontaneity.

Living on the edge.

Constant risk, constant change.

Unpredictable.

But what's the appeal of that?

You have no control over it.

You're still passive, only in a different way.

•　•　•

Some people find it stimulating.

These are people who thought life was boring.

Who got stuck in the rut of one moment after another.

Who let themselves drift through that drift.

Who couldn't resist it.

They need to acquiesce.

. . .

But these are not my problems.

People think I'm passive.

This is a misconception.

I never thought of myself as passive.

I stayed in my room and tried to feel time.

Experience the present.

Get as close to it as I could.

And stay in control.

Like a scientist in a lab, I had to control the conditions.

I had to sit there, I had to be alone.

I had to reside inside my mind.

So I could examine it.

So I could take it apart.

So I could see how time was composed and how it felt.

And stay in control.

. . .

This wasn't passive.

It was the opposite.

People have missed this point.

I was trying to fight passivity.

To exert control over myself.

Over my surroundings.

Over my mind and my memories.

Over my work.

Over the passing of time.

. . .

I failed.

I proved you can't do it.

You can't find a present moment.

No matter how hard you try.

You can't control everything.

No matter how hard you try.

Both will elude you.

At the same time, in the same way, and with equal certainty.

I wasted so much time.

I can't get it back.

I see it now.

And it's too late.

· · ·

Some people like everything changing.

Without warning.

Other people like facing the collapse of presence.

They find it bracing.

A slap in the face.

No more illusions.

The end of pretend.

They feel they're living truthfully.

If you call it living.

It's ironic.

You're living out of step with time.

Yet you're living for the first time correctly aligned with time.

· · ·

Some people think it's great.

It's not that I don't.

But I've spent so much time on these issues.

Wasted my life on them.

Now I have to waste eternity.

What a disappointment.

I'd like to move on.

· · ·

They sent me to talk to Stanislavsky.

They thought he might cheer me up.

It turned out we had a lot in common.

More than you might have thought.

He thinks actors need to use their lives.

You try to be someone else by remembering things about yourself.

You bring your past into the present.

You feel it again.

Reexperience it.

You pretend to play a role.

While really you're playing yourself.

· · ·

Acting becomes not the representation of a character.

But the re-presentation of your self.

The role is a vehicle to re-present your life.

Of course, all our lives are re-presentations.

From moment to moment.

So acting offers a double re-presentation.

A representation of re-presentation.

A demonstration of how we produce life in general.

Acting voraciously cannibalizes the actor's life.

Nothing is off-limits.

Everything leaves itself open for appropriation.

All that matters is the result.

Everything must be sacrificed.

· · ·

Of course, nothing was there in the first place.

So the performance constructs a phantom.

A ghostly double of the actor's life.

It's the same as how you constructed the first feeling.

It just happens later.

Further away from the sensation you're reconstructing.

A distance significant only in the regime of linear time.

Which is a fiction.

Either way it's the same operation.

The actor eats his life alive.

. . .

Representation as cannibalization.

That's what we have in common.

Stanislavsky was lucid and stern about this.

The actor has to relinquish everything.

To the integrity of the product.

Make a commitment.

Shear away the distractions.

The excess, the waste.

The inessential.

Allow the representation to get as close as possible.

Fuse what you call past into what you call present.

Push them as asymptotically near each other as you can.

Approximate the proximate.

. . .

The performance becomes a transparency.

A palimpsest that presents re-presentation.

Brings it forward.

Teases it out of hiding.

Makes it show its colors.

Under the sign of the cannibal.

Who devours everything in sight.

And effaces the traces.

. . .

Stanislavsky sees that life is about use.

That's why I can relate to him.

Benjamin thinks it's about losing the moment.

Pater thinks it's about savoring the moment.

Stanislavsky appreciates that it's about what can be used.

Making-present is a process of use.

A frantic attempt to save everything.

Salvage the waste.

Put each moment to use.

Like a pathological pack rat preserving every scrap.

· · ·

Pleasure, loss, the Messiah.

Whatever.

The point is to do something.

Don't just sit there watching it go away.

Everything goes through the machine of making-present.

It's indiscriminate.

Once you get past that, what's worth using?

What do you want to feel again?

What will repay the cost of salvage?

· · ·

It's not easy.

That's why I had to sit still.

Concentrate.

Control my environment.

Every minute there's another minute.

You're not going to stop them.

It takes will, effort, focus.

You have to really want it.

It weeds things out.

What's worth the effort of cannibalization?

What can you really use?

That's what my work was about.

That's what Stanislavsky was trying to teach his students.

Focus on what you can use.

Control the chaos.

•   •   •

F I V E

Boredom

In his 1938 painting *The Sublime Moment,* Salvador Dali depicted a barren landscape not unlike that of his more famous bent-watch painting, *The Persistence of Memory.* Into this space Dali placed a dilapidated phone receiver growing out of a tree, a snail crawling over a tree branch toward this receiver, and a drop of water hanging over a razor blade, itself perched over a dish of fried eggs. The drop of water clearly instantiates an ephemeral moment; the fried eggs do too. But this image generates its title's momentary sublime only in the context of the Surrealist thought from which Dali opportunistically drew. From the Surrealist perspective, the seemingly random juxtaposition of scattered elements defined a moment and embodied the moment's potential for both sublimity and defamiliarization. Such artist-critics as André Breton, Max Ernst, Pierre Reverdy, Antonin Artaud, Germaine Dulac, and Jean Epstein derived their notions of surreal experience from the power of the momentary and ephemeral. Surreal experience occurred in the moment of shocking, random juxtaposition in which one plane of reality rudely intersects another. This clash creates a new "reality" from the unique combination of its two elements. "The surrealist aim," as Mary Ann Caws puts it, "could be loosely defined as the intention of transforming (with all the deliberately alchemical force which attaches to the latter verb) sets of static polar contraries into potentially powerful juxtapositions, intellectually uncomfortable to contemplate, shocking to the normal perception in their intense irrationality." [1]

For Surrealist critics, the model of this startling moment of arbitrary juxtaposition had been provided in the Comte de Lautréamont's late-nineteenth-century *Chants de Maldoror,* in which Lautréamont, the pseudonym of Isidore Ducasse, coined the phrase "as beautiful as the chance meeting on an operating table of a sewing machine and an umbrella." [2] Lautréamont's formulation emphasized not just this momentary encounter's arbitrary nature but also its beauty and its composition from mundane icons of daily life. The surreal moment carves an unexpected instant of radiance from the otherwise uninteresting components of everyday life. It forms in this way a hybrid of a sublime moment and a defamiliarizing moment. The surreal moment sets itself against the unthinking drift of everyday life in an effort to shock habituated modern subjects into recognizing the allure of random encounters and the untapped potential of taken-for-granted daily objects. As Caws indicates, we must "go so far as to associate the *point sublime* with the contrary and yet intimately connected notion of *ennui,* that is, to insist that exaltation is always accompanied by tedium" (34). In Surrealist conceptions of the moment—that is, in Surrealism itself, which pivoted on the shocking moment of arbitrary juxtaposition—the point of sublime beauty was predicated against the drift of everyday life. The surreal moment could be shocking only against the background of the undifferentiated perceptions around it.

The work of André Breton, Surrealism's leading writer and theorist, specified four progressive categories of momentary experience. All forms of the moment generate from the basic moment of encounter, in which one element simply and neutrally meets another. As in Lautréamont's "chance meeting," this montage moment forms the heart of Surrealist practice. Breton exemplified this moment of encounter as the conjunction of planets in astrology. References to astrological conjunctions occur throughout Breton's works, above all in *Mad Love,* where they recur as off-the-cuff instances of the moment of encounter: for instance, "Whether or not it results from the conjunction of Venus with Mars at a particular place in the sky of my birth, I have all too often felt the bad effects of discord in the very inside of love." Planetary conjunctions instantiated Breton's notion that a momentary encounter could generate long-term consequences. "On April 20, 1934, at the height of the 'occultation' of Venus by the moon (this occurrence only supposed to happen once in the year), I was having lunch in a little restaurant rather unfortunately situated near the entrance of a cemetery," he writes, in a sentence that specified a moment four ways: a date, an astrological conjunction, an annual event, and a location in time and place.[3]

The astrological moment signaled Breton's interest in the moment of encounter as a generative principle of daily life. It only made sense that a universe constituted by moments of encounter would be regulated by celestial moments of encounter. But the moment of encounter acquired purpose primarily by forging a sublime moment in which the subject would be transported by intense evanescent feeling. The sublime moment generally occurs as the "spark" produced by an unexpected moment of encounter; the unexpectedness heightens both the intensity and the ephemerality of the sublime response. Stumbling in the course of daily life across an unanticipated configuration of elements, the subject is without warning seized by acute feeling that fleetingly removes him or her from the drift of daily experience.

In so doing, the sublime moment creates the possibility of moments of self-observation. Set apart from the flow of daily life, this moment provides the potential for self-examination, as if the self were momentarily detached from itself in order to observe its own actions. The moment of self-observation is by definition a defamiliarizing moment, and it expressed Surrealism's didactic aim to change the way people perceived themselves and their environment. The Surrealist work of art endeavored to show its viewers an alternate reality, a sur-reality, that would shake up their perceptions, refresh their awareness, and create moments of productive self-analysis.

Yet Breton's vision of Surrealism also aimed toward a fourth moment, a hypothetical, future utopian moment that would unite and resolve oppositions and contradictions. As he wrote in the Second

Manifesto of Surrealism, "Everything tends to make us believe that there exists a certain point of the mind at which life and death, the real and the imagined, past and future, the communicable and the incommunicable, high and low, cease to be perceived as contradictions. . . . [O]ne will never find any other motivating force in the activities of the Surrealists than the hope of finding and fixing this point."[4] This moment of reconciliation operated in Breton's writing as a horizon, a final destination that in theory provides the ultimate moment of juxtaposition, bringing together all possible contradictions in a frenzy of encounter. True to the manifesto's idealistic quality, this potential functioned less as a concrete reality than as a mystical potential moment, an almost theological vision of redemption on Surrealist terms of juxtaposition and sublimity.

Breton's clearest formulation of the centrality to his thought of the momentary encounter occurred in the opening sentence of the astrologically titled *Signe ascendant:* "For me the only evidence in the world is given by the spontaneous, extra-lucid, insolent relationship, which common sense would shrink from confronting, established under certain conditions between one thing and another."[5] This sort of relationship can occur between elements in art, between people who suddenly encounter each other, or between planets in the sky, whose random meetings astrology aspires to render meaningful. "What do you consider the essential encounter of your life?" Breton and Paul Eluard asked in a questionnaire. "To what extent did this encounter seem to you, and does it seem to you now, to be fortuitous or foreordained?" (19). The "manifest insufficiency" of the responses Breton and Eluard received did not minimize the significance of these questions as statements of Breton's interest in the moment of encounter as the conjunction of past and future. In *Communicating Vessels,* Breton narrated an emblematic encounter on the human plane:

On April 5, 1931, toward noon, in a café on the Place Blanche where my friends and I usually met, I had just told Paul Eluard my night dream (the one about the hashish), and we were about to finish interpreting it with his help—for he had observed how I had spent most of my time the day before—when my gaze met that of a young woman or girl, seated with a man a few steps from us.[6]

In this long sentence, delineating date, time, and place, Breton took pains to establish the specificity of the unique present moment in which he found himself. These specifications are not, however, precise: the time is toward noon, and the place, located by street, is "a café" with no name. The coyness about details cleverly demonstrates that a present moment can be neither lived nor reconstructed. The present moment can be only approximated, circled around. "Toward noon" holds out the possibility of precision only to snatch it away; it captures in two words the present's slippage toward the future. Whatever exact time circumscribed the described moment ceases to matter, for that time was always already sliding "toward noon."

This teasing combination of precision and imprecision marks most of the sentence's details. Its present moment occurs between the past event of having just told Eluard the dream and the future event of being just about to interpret it. Even here Breton avoids exactness: he says that he "had just told" Eluard his dream but also that they "were about to finish interpreting it." The start of the interpretation is explicitly elided, as if to reinforce the partial nature of both the reconstructive narration and the putatively present moment. The apparent particularity of "the one about the hashish" evaporates once we realize that we are excluded from this reference, which therefore remains opaque despite its seeming specificity. "Where my friends and I usually met" similarly gestures toward habitual action while leaving the location vague and the event ("usually") unpredictable.

This mixture of times and tenses demonstrates the kind of angled confrontations between different dimensions that Breton promoted as the heart of Surrealist thought. These calculatedly inexact encounters provide the backdrop for the precisely momentary meeting of the sentence's denouement: the instant in which Breton's gaze meets "that of a young woman or girl, seated with a man a few steps from us." The matching of gazes, especially between a man and a woman, emblematizes the moment of encounter conceived by Breton. The flash of human encounter literally brings together in unexpected juxtaposition two alien and unconnected realities. Yet no sooner has Breton supplied this instant than he extends its duration: "I surveyed her from head to toe at my leisure, or perhaps it was that suddenly I could no longer detach my gaze from her." The ensuing description reaffirms the momentary charge of the first encounter, whose erotic energy is generated as the spark thrown off by the unanticipated meeting. While Breton remains fascinated by the woman, everything that follows can be only a falloff from the intensity of the initial encounter.

In this way, the erotic encounter can become more tangible than the factual configuration of planets in the sky. It becomes a sublime encounter, a moment in which powerful feeling lifts the participants out of the ordinary life around them. In *Mad Love,* Breton called this fleeting moment "convulsive beauty":

> The word "convulsive," which I use to describe the only beauty which should concern us, would lose any meaning in my eyes were it to be conceived in motion and not at the exact expiration of this motion. There can be no beauty at all, as far as I am concerned—convulsive beauty—except at the cost of affirming the reciprocal relations linking the object seen in its motion and in its repose. (10)

For Breton, beauty could arise only in a fleeting and momentary form. We recognize it from the contrast between continuity and stasis, between the sublime moment and the ordinary life around it. The drift of quotidian experience provides the background for the sublime moment as both sublime and momentary. Near the end of the Second Manifesto, Breton made clear the importance of this sublime moment for a Surrealism that "believes, and it will never believe in anything more wholeheartedly, in reproducing artificially this ideal moment when man, in the grips of a particular emotion, is suddenly seized by this something 'stronger than himself'" (161–62). Intense ecstatic feeling marks off a moment distinct from the flow of everyday life, and the category of the moment circularly provides a repository for that intensity of feeling.

Breton insisted that this surreal moment must remain a purely emotional experience. He differentiated this view from that of poet Pierre Reverdy, who in his 1918 essay "L'image" had first advanced the concept of random juxtaposition, explicitly connecting it to the production of images.[7] "One creates . . . a strong image," wrote Reverdy, "in bringing together without comparison two distant realities of which the mind alone has grasped the relations." An image is defined as that which holds in place the moment at which one "reality" unexpectedly crosses paths with another. The image, Reverdy suggested, "is born not from a comparison but from the bringing together of two more or less distanced realities." The image cannot acquire poetic power from two realities that are opposites, as they will simply repel each other. The two realities must have some relation to each other to be able to approach each other productively. "An image is not strong," Reverdy emphasized, "because it is brutal or fantastic—but because the association of ideas is remote and exact. The result obtained immediately stabilizes the rightness of the association."

For Breton, Reverdy's specifications indicated too much "premeditation." "In my opinion," he wrote in the first Manifesto of Surrealism, "it is erroneous to claim that 'the mind has grasped the relationship' of two realities in the presence of each other" (36). In apprehending the juxtaposition of two realities, the mind, Breton argued, "has seized nothing consciously. It is, as it were, from the fortuitous juxtaposition of the two terms that a particular light has sprung, the light of the image" (37). What Breton called the Surrealist image arose from the fleeting light produced in a unique juxtaposition, an instantaneous chemical reaction that he went on to call a spark: "Now, it is not within man's power, so far as I can tell, to effect the juxtaposition of two realities so far apart. We are therefore obliged to admit that the two terms of the image are not deduced one from the other by the mind for the specific purpose of producing the spark, . . . reason's role being limited to taking note of, and appreciating, the luminous phenomenon." The subject's "reason" can only stand back and "appreciate" the sensation of the sublime moment. Cognitive awareness can be assigned no "role" beyond this accounting of sensual response. For Breton, this emotive reaction locates the heart "of the activity I call Surrealist."

• • •

What does it mean to be bored?

We think we know it when we see it, but what does it mean?

What is the range of feelings we mean to encompass with this word?

How do they overlap with other feelings?

All fascinating questions.

But in the empty moment, the question changes.

What does it mean not to be bored?

• • •

I've been spending time showing Saussure around.

We started in the nineteenth century, wandering the Paris streets.

That's what people did back then.

I didn't see the thrill.

You see how hard people work not to be bored.

They want to make something out of every moment.

This was where it started, I told him, the modern mania always to be looking at something, feeling something, going somewhere.

Baron Haussmann thought he was just widening the streets, firming up the boulevards, getting the city clear and organized.

By giving people all this space to walk in and all these sight lines to peer down, he wrought all the boredom of modernity.

Once people saw that there were all these things to do and see, all these places to go, they understood that they could also be bored.

Boring compared to what?

• • •

This is the problem with Bergson.

Bergson is boring.

It's just one moment after another, droning on and on and on, monotonous, uninflected.

He sees it himself, because he starts protesting too much in defending duration against the thrill of sensual moments: "Discontinuous though they appear, however, in point of fact they stand out against the continuity of a background on which they are designed, and to which indeed they owe the intervals that separate them; they are the beats of the drum which breaks forth here and there in the symphony."

He's taking it personally, getting defensive: "Our attention fixes on them because they interest it more," he acknowledges about discrete moments, "but each of them is borne by the fluid mass of our whole psychical existence. Each is only the best illuminated point of a moving zone which comprises all that we feel or think or will—all, in short, that we are at any given moment. It is this entire zone which in reality makes up our state. Now, states thus defined cannot be regarded as distinct elements. They continue each other in an endless flow."

We get the point.

He's addled enough to mix his metaphors.

•   •   •

Bergson's so locked into the logic of linear time that he sees only these two extremes: either duration or discrete moments.

And he even gives in on that point.

Can't we all just get along?

He doesn't deny that we perceive isolated moments.

He just says that even if we do, they occur only against the background of duration, which drones on and on and on in spite of everything, oblivious.

Well, ok, sure.

But then who cares about duration?

It becomes equivalent to everything.

It doesn't stop anything from happening or cause anything to happen or have any implications or consequences.

It's there.

Granted.

I guess Bergson wanted everyone to like him.

Is duration boring because it's self-evident?

You say like everyone that an hour lasts sixty minutes, that the minute is worth sixty seconds.

You therefore believe in duration.

You cannot speak without using all the adverbs, all the words that evoke what endures, what passes, what one waits for. . . .

Duration is in grammar, in morphology as well as in syntax.

It is not really an ingredient of acts; in the psychological realm . . . it plays no role; we can eliminate it.

Gaston Bachelard said all these things in the 1930s.

He hated Bergson.

He writes about him like a spurned lover.

We took this duration, without discussion, as the only quality of time, as a synonym for time. Let us recognize it: it is only a postulate. . . . But we always have the right a priori to start from a different postulate and to attempt a new construction in which duration is derived and not postulated.

•   •   •

Bergson and Bachelard have this love/hate thing because they're locked into the same rut of presence.

Bachelard's cure is worse than the disease.

Time has only one reality, that of the Instant.

He makes such a good case against Bergson. He's so close.

The line that brings together the points and that schematizes duration is only a panoramic and retrospective function . . . subjective, indirect, and secondary.

Duration is only a construction, without any absolute reality.

It is fashioned from the outside, by memory; it epitomizes the power of imagination, which wants to dream and relive the past, but not comprehend.

Right on.

Except that all these things are just as true of the momentary instants that Bachelard wants to valorize in duration's stead.

Consciousness is consciousness of the instant and consciousness of the instant is consciousness.

He takes the cake for self-delusion.

He talks about the instant as if it's a can of soda he can put his hands around.

They deserve each other.

·   ·   ·

Bachelard says that duration doesn't work because you have to step outside duration to formulate duration.

"To think about time is to frame life."

That sounds clever, but of course it's wrong.

You don't have to get off a train to know you're riding on it.

Or, to be fair, it's only partly right. Bachelard has a solid intuition, but he can't formulate it correctly because it would call into question his own ideas.

The problem with duration isn't presenting it as continuous but presenting it as simply knowable.

You can know duration only as a re-presentation of something that's already happened.

But re-presentation and duration are mutually exclusive.

It's not "an endless flow," as Bergson says, because it's jagged, asymmetrical; it's all sorts of different levels of construction and reconstruction, crowding in and jostling for position all at once.

Just saying this makes it knowable, translatable.

·   ·   ·

Bachelard seems to sense this, but unfortunately it's no more or less true for his vision of palpable instants.

This shows you the drawback of being stuck in the rut of presence.

Both of them keep having to confront the disparities between their theories and everything else they have to account for. Bergson winds up with a theory so neutral and inclusive that it effaces itself into immateriality; Bachelard barters away the strength of his bitter critique by staking out the equally wrongheaded extreme.

This is my point: they're two peas on opposite sides of the pod of presence.

•   •   •

Both of them had the same problem with duration.

They both thought it was boring.

The same thing again and again and again.

The antipathy to boring duration led them both astray.

Bergson gets himself tangled up trying to account for all the sensations that are not durational.

Bachelard falls for the lure of the sensual moment, so much more exciting than pure negativity.

He wrote in a more sober mood:

"For us, all the energetic judgments—that is, all the judgments that engage consciousness—are negative judgments."

He's contradicting his infatuation with positive instants, but he's starting to get at something.

He doesn't just advance the negative as a corollary to the positive; he grasps the in-between.

He says, "We distinguish the traits of a phenomenon only by differentiations," and those distinctions can only occupy the chasms between the positive and negative terms.

"From the functional point-of-view, there is nothing more normal, nothing more necessary, than . . . the easing of the function, the resting of the function, the non-functioning of the function, since the function, from all evidence, must often interrupt itself to function."

It's a start.

•   •   •

Bachelard gets away from simple presence—even though he also endorses it—by advocating this uneasy, unpredictable, up-and-down kind of presence.

It seems like a contradiction for him to endorse a tangible present, a forceful negativity, and a peaks-and-valleys rhythm. But these three ideas are not mutually exclusive if you see his books not as a model of presence, not as a rebuke to Bergson, but as what they really are: a theory of how to avoid being bored.

That's Bachelard's secret agenda.

He's restless, nervous; he can't keep still.

He wants to gobble up every instant, nothing's enough for him, he's never sated.

He wants to feel each present, get inside it, know it intimately.

He wants to get inside the underside too.

He's a glutton, a hidden hedonist, a secret sensualist.

You can tell he's serious about it because he's really thought it out. That's what seems contradictory but isn't.

Because he sees that you escape boredom only against the background of boredom, by accepting it, letting it in, working with it.

He sees that you can be bored—or not—only by comparison.

And if you're stuck in the rut of one moment after another, you can't break out to pleasure.

•   •   •

Benjamin felt this boredom too.

You see it in the cracks of his writing: he talks about the constant, sudden change in a movie, about its shock effect, about how the mechanically reproduced work of art generates an infinity of copies, all the same, one after another.

When he says that the nonreproduced artwork has an aura, what he means is it's not boring.

The presence of the artwork is tied up to its nonboringness, and that package is called aura.

The artwork isn't boring because it's unique, because it carries its baggage, because it aggressively marks its place in time and space.

Mechanical reproduction is boring because it's the same thing over and over again.

A movie has to keep jostling the viewer, changing and jumping away every moment, just to keep you interested.

"The painting invites the spectator to contemplation; before it the spectator can abandon himself to his associations.

"Before the movie frame he cannot do so."

Paradoxically, the static artwork allows the viewer to drift, while the jumpy, shifty movie pins the viewer into a rut of presents, one after another, methodical and predictable.

The movie has to keep distracting your attention from the looming threat of boredom.

• • •

Re-presentation is boring.

It flattens everything out.

The machine of re-presentation makes everything equal.

Once your own experience is held away from you, why would it hold your interest?

Why not just watch television?

If there's no longer any difference, if you're as distanced from your experience as from the experiences of others, as from the experiences you watch, if everything is leveled out, why stay interested?

In the empty moment you can't get bored.

Things are changing all the time; there's always something else to do.

We eliminated the valleys.

We took advantage of time's distraction from itself.

We caught the moment while it wasn't looking.

• • •

We don't show movies here.

They don't work in this context.

Movies rely on that peaks-and-valleys energy, the roller-coaster highs and
low lulls.

We want to force people to get over that.

We want to iron out the oscillations.

In the empty moment, you can't keep being batted back and forth like
the ball in a pinball machine.

You have to focus, stay alert, watch for sudden shifts.

You can't be bored because you can't rely on the empty moment as a space
of contrast between being bored and being something else.

You're inside that empty moment.

You lose that extremity of emotion.

You need the empty moment as the terrace on which you step outside for
a respite from the emotions, to gather your feelings, to figure out what
you're feeling, how it's moving.

To feel these emotions, you need to be able to step outside them.

So the empty moment flattens it out a little.

Nothing comes free.

• • •

If you don't understand what this is like, you might think it means that
the empty moment is boring.

Far from it.

You've lost the safe haven that gives you a breather from your raw self.

You have to face it.

Moment after moment after moment.

It's all you've got, and you're finally free to confront it.

Except that you don't face it and you don't confront it; you've traded in
those options so that you can live inside it.

It's liberating, but I won't deny that people find it hard to get used to.

• • •

So you see we do what we can to keep people from getting bored.

Movies don't work because they're all about the spaces; to watch a movie,
you have to get inside the empty moments.

Television works better.

But basically we try to blur these distinctions entirely.

Because we've acknowledged it's all the same.

We've stopped trying to enforce these arbitrary boundaries.

If you're not living life, if you're no longer in that zone of presence, you don't have to make logical contortions to privilege it any more.

You can stop pretending that what you call your experience of what you call your real life can be considered any different from what you call your experience of what you call tv or movies.

Get a life, the saying goes.

People say it's a waste of time to spend too much of it watching movies or tv.

It's all about this desperation about waste and loss and death.

Illogical ideas get advanced and accepted because everyone's so panicked about seizing every minute before it ends.

• • •

It's liberating to give up this nonsensical effort to police discriminations among types of experience.

You'd be surprised.

You don't need presence.

You don't need to privilege your "own" experience of your "own" body.

You don't own anything.

In giving it up, you get it back.

Be careful what you wish for.

In the empty moment, you'll see what it's like to live inside the unprocessed experience of your own body.

That's what you wanted?

You've got it.

See how you like it.

• • •

Instead of encouraging people to watch movies or tv, we've gone one step further.

We re-create that experience for them.

We aim to please.

We're trying to get people to concentrate on the experience of their
bodies; we're not hemmed in by linear time.

So we like to shake things up a little.

After all, what's mooring one moment to the next?

Moments succeed or precede each other based only on this made-up
story about linear durational time.

There's no reason they have to.

We eliminate the waste.

Maximize each moment.

Leave out the boring ones.

Some people find it strenuous and wearing.

We try to screen those people out before we start.

• • •

People complain that they can't get distracted in the empty moment.

They're missing the point: there's no longer anything to be distracted from.

In life you have to distract yourself from the boredom of linear time.

In life time is distracted from itself.

In life the body is distracted from itself.

Here you can rest, you can center yourself, you can focus.

Obviously, you can't do that inside linear time.

So you can't have it both ways.

• • •

In the nineteenth century, people were so desperate for distraction that
they started wandering the streets.

The flâneurs of nineteenth-century Paris tried to outrun their own bodies,
defeat their own distraction from themselves by walking further and
further, faster and faster, taking in more and more of the things around
them.

As if they could catch up on presence by moving fast enough.

As if they could sneak up on self-presence by darting around a corner
   and overtaking it by surprise.
They were frantically trying to keep themselves amused, keep moving,
   find new things to experience.
They started riding bicycles, taking trains.
They were distracting themselves from self-distraction.
Not long afterward they started going to the movies.

• • •

Surrealism and Cinema

For the Surrealists, it was above all the cinema that possessed the
uncanny ability to penetrate the surface of the world and encapsulate in moments of shocking in-sight the nature of the physical
and sensual universe.[8] "What is clear," wrote Antonin Artaud in an
essay on cinema, "is what is immediately accessible, but what is
immediately accessible is the mere skin of life. We soon realise that
this over-familiar life which has lost all its symbols is not the whole
of life."[9] Cinema could literalize and visualize the surreal impetus
to get beneath the surface of the world and pierce the habitualiz-
ing rituals that make opaque the richness of material phenomena.
"The cinema is surrealist in its essence," writes Ado Kyrou in his
analysis of Surrealism and film. Going on, Kyrou encapsulates the
surreal imperative of defamiliarization:

> What is more deceiving than life? . . . Incontestably our senses
> are incomplete and we see, we touch, we feel things that are
> much more than we believe them to be. Life forms sinuous
> folds that hide certain parts of itself. . . . cinema can show all
> that. . . . And that is much more true than daily life; that is real.
> The whole tree with its mysteries, in its time and in its space, is
> present, just as the lamp in the middle of the street is present.[10]

As in Kyrou's invocation of the tree and the lamp, this defamiliarizing imperative expressed itself in isolated moments through the
immanent power of discrete objects, which become fully present
by revealing themselves on screen. "Even the most arid and banal

image is transformed when it is projected on the screen," wrote Artaud. "The smallest detail, the most insignificant object assume a meaning and a life which pertain to them alone" (66). This presence arises not accidentally but as the by-product of the intersection between film's clarifying power and the masked realities of the daily world: "By being isolated, the objects obtain a life of their own which becomes increasingly independent and detaches them from their usual meaning. A leaf, a bottle, a hand, etc., live with an almost animal life which is crying out to be used." Guillaume Apollinaire made this same point in writing that "almost no one knows how to see the beauty of things the cinema sometimes forces one to see." [11]

The cinema's ability to provide these detached, uncanny images of objects indicated not just its "essence" and not just its defamiliarizing power but above all its supernatural quality. "Essentially," Artaud suggested, "the cinema reveals a whole occult life with which it puts us directly into contact" (66). The cinema becomes super-natural by providing momentary insights into the natural world. In Jean Epstein's view, this access to supernatural insight occurs automatically in the momentary conjunction of natural phenomena and the film camera, as the "click of a shutter makes a *photogénie* which did not exist before it." [12] The in-sight of the camera lens brings out of objects their essence. "Our eye, without very long practice, cannot discover it directly. A lens centers it, drains it, and distills *photogénie* between its focal planes" (91). Because, in the mechanically reproduced image, we resee something familiar, the re-production allows us to focus on new qualities; re-presentation elicits something that our habituated perceptions could not discover on their own. "On screen," notes Epstein, "we re-see what the cinema has already seen once" (91).

This conception of the filmic moment as both sublime and defamiliarizing emerged in the writings of Germaine Dulac, one of the primary filmmakers working in the Surrealists' epistemological atmosphere. "One of [film's] first characteristics," Dulac wrote, "is its educational and instructive power; in documentaries we see film as a sort of microscope with which we are able to perceive, within the realm of reality, things we would not perceive without it. . . . With cinema," she continued, "no more unexplored countries! No

125

more barriers between us and things! . . . The cinema is an eye wide open on life, an eye more powerful than our own and which sees things we cannot see. . . . it teaches us things which, without it, we would not know." [13]

In these exhortations, Dulac sounds remarkably like Dziga Vertov, the Soviet filmmaker who also, in this period, reveled in film's ability to "put together any given points in the universe, no matter where I've recorded them." [14] Calling his new form of cinema "kino-eye," Vertov writes: "Kino-eye pursues precisely this goal of establishing a visual bond between the workers of the whole world" (52); and "Kino-eye is the documentary cinematic decoding of both the visual world and that which is invisible to the naked eye. Kino-eye means the conquest of space, the visual linkage of people throughout the entire world" (87). Vertov also echoes Dulac's remark in "Essence of the Cinema" that "scientifically, cinema casts upon everything it records a clear light which banishes errors and distortions" (39). Kino-eye, Vertov proposes, "leads to the creation of a fresh perception of the world. I decipher in a new way a world unknown to you" (18). This effort aspires to use film technique to reveal what Vertov unflinchingly called "truth": "Not kino-eye for its own sake, but truth through the means and possibilities of film-eye, i.e., *kinopravda* [film-truth]. . . . Kino-eye as the possibility of making the invisible visible, the unclear clear, the hidden manifest, the disguised overt, the acted nonacted; making falsehood into truth . . . an attempt to show the truth on the screen—Film-truth" (41–42).

Yet Dulac ultimately moved away from this sense of the film "eye" as a defamiliarizing moment toward a view of the film moment as an ineffable visual impression that would enhance the viewer's soul. Whereas Vertov wanted to use form to reveal truth, Dulac aimed to overwhelm the viewer with the pure form of the image. For Vertov, this revelation was ultimately a rational, ideological "truth" leading toward revolution. For Dulac, the emphasis remained not on Vertov's "clear" truth but on the sensuous possibilities opened up by immersion in cinema's visuality. If this experience leads the viewer to understand the "truth" of life's mystery and richness, so much the better. But Dulac emphasized not the distant future rewards offered by a political aesthetic but a hedonistic immersion in the present tense of experience. In this sense, Dulac's brief foray into Vertovian "educational and instructive" power was a false trail, as the main theme of her aesthetic set itself against the Vertovian urge to make "the invisible visible, the unclear clear, the hidden manifest, the disguised overt." Dulac wanted to keep the invisible invisible, the unclear unclear, and the hidden hidden. Like her colleague Jean Epstein, Dulac hoped to use the ineffability of the cinematic image to point toward the realms of the unknown and mysterious to which we generally remain blind. "The cinema," as Epstein wrote, "is supernatural in its essence" (93).

Writing in the early years of cinema, Dulac wanted to grasp the "essence of cinema," the properties that characterized it as a new medium different from the media that preceded it. For Dulac, this distinctiveness resided in both film's pedagogical imperative and its ability to use fleeting impressions to evoke and enhance the viewer's soulful sensibilities. "The great pity, as far as film is concerned," she began a 1928 essay, "is that, though a uniquely visual art, it does not at present seek its emotion in the pure optic sense. Every cinematic drama . . . *must* be visual and not literary. . . . the power of the image alone should be the active principle and take precedence over every other quality."[15] We see the Surrealist influence when Dulac writes in this same essay that "a real film can't be able to be told, since it must draw its active and emotive principle from images formed of unique visual tones. Can you tell a painting? Can you tell a sculpture? . . . as cinema stands today, a blind man could take pleasure in a filmed work. . . . the story is nothing. The story is a surface" (33–34).

Dulac recognized that this cinema was a utopian aspiration: "Our ideal is far beyond our accomplishments; you must help us to liberate the cinema from its shackles and create a pure cinema" (42). But in speaking of what "pure cinema" might achieve, Dulac took recourse in the analogy of music in a way that revealed her desire to evoke "states of the soul." "Only music can inspire this feeling which cinema also aspires to" (41), she suggested in "The Essence of the Cinema," because it too creates an abstract system that aims to evoke emotion in the receiver. "There is no story there except that

127

of a soul which feels and thinks, and nevertheless our feelings are reached," she wrote of pieces by Debussy and Chopin which "are the expressions of a soul pouring forth, reacting among things" (41).

When Dulac, then, wrote that "visual impact is ephemeral, it's an impression you receive and which suggests a thousand thoughts" (34), she clarified three components of the viewer's drift: the viewer remains free to experience "a thousand thoughts" that the film can inspire but not regulate; the film's visuals create an impression that manifests itself only in the viewer's experience; and film's visuals are ephemeral, always moving and changing, making the viewer's experience a process of impressionistic, even subliminal reactions. In cinema, Dulac recognized, neither the sublime moment nor the defamiliarizing moment could stay still. They could exist solely as fleeting impressions, tangible instances of that "convulsive beauty" which can appear only on the ground of its own disappearance.

Montage as Epistemology: Ernst and Eisenstein

As Dulac's writings began to indicate, cinema's mobile sensations required a view of spectatorship more complex than Breton's conception of transporting sublimity. This broader vision, which I will elaborate in the film theory of Sergei Eisenstein, also originated in Max Ernst's writings in the 1930s on *collage* and *frottage* (rubbing), which exploited Breton's formulation of the convulsive moment to produce a model of the montage moment as an epistemological upheaval. Ernst's theory of collage-as-epistemology drew on the Breton/Reverdy idea of the imagistic moment as what Ernst called "the chance meeting of two distant realities on an unfamiliar plane." Yet Ernst went further than either Breton or Reverdy in expanding the consequences of this fleeting instant both epistemologically and dialectically. For Ernst, the moment of collision generates a third quality as the product of its unique combination of elements. As in Eisenstein's cinematic montage, this third quality gives the montage moment a dialectical dimension and pushes it forward, into motion, through the viewer's response.[16]

Ernst most fully theorized this aesthetic in two essays, the brief "Comment on force l'inspiration" ("How One Forces Inspiration"), published in 1933 in the Surrealist journal *Le Surréalisme au service de la revolution,* and the longer "Au delà de la peinture" ("Beyond Painting") in a 1936 issue of *Cahiers d'art.*[17] At the simplest level, collage epitomized the Surrealist logic of surprising juxtapositions. "One might define collage," Ernst wrote about his technique, "as an alchemy resulting from the unexpected meeting of two or more heterogeneous elements" (B, 16). The collage, for Ernst, provides a surface on which juxtaposition can occur. Yet through the discovery of *frottage,* Ernst moved beyond this analogy to conceive his aesthetic as an interlocking series of epiphanic moments. The discovery of the momentary *frottage* technique was itself momentary. "Finding myself one rainy evening in a seaside inn," Ernst made drawings from wooden boards "by placing on them, at random, sheets of paper which I undertook to rub with black lead." On observing these rubbings, Ernst reports, "I was surprised by the sudden intensification of my visionary capacities and by the hallucinatory succession of contradictory images superimposed, one upon the other, with the persistence and rapidity characteristic of amorous memories" (B, 7). From this time, he tells us, he grasped the link between the aesthetic form of the moment and the subjective experience of the moment. The moment of "inspiration" could be "forced."

For Ernst, the discovery of *frottage* gave the artist a technique equivalent to the Surrealists' automatic writing, in which the writer transcribed the free flow of her or his thoughts. This process, based in the free association of Freudian analysis, enabled the writer, as if in a trance, to stand outside her or his subconscious thoughts. As an artistic practice, it thus gave writers a distance from their own works. Ernst conceived this possibility of self-removal as a series of momentary experiences. The artist, first, occupies a self-conscious space apart from the drift of the everyday world. He or she then composes an artificial field of intersections that allows the viewer to achieve that same level of momentary in-sight. Coming full circle, the artist can stand back from his or her creation and reexperience the feeling of distance that first inspired it.

"It is as a spectator," Ernst suggested, "that the author, indifferent or passionate, attends the birth of his work and watches the

phases of its development" (B, 8).[18] The artist's position in relation
to the collage reflects the possibility of self-distance embodied in
the experience of the moment. Inspiration makes the artist feel like
a bystander to the act of creation. More specifically, the moment of
the artist's self-distance parallels the real-world moment of the startling intersection of realities, which in turn parallels the moment of
image memorialized in the collage's aesthetic juxtapositions. In the
face of the moment of startling reality, which will be imitated by
the juxtapositions that compose the collage, the artist experiences
his or her own moment of epiphanic removal. Ernst wrote:

> In finding myself more and more engrossed in this activity
> (passivity) which later came to be called "critical paranoia," . . .
> and in striving more and more to restrain my own active
> participation in the unfolding of the picture and, finally, by
> widening in this way the active part of the mind's hallucina-
> tory faculties I came to attend *as spectator* the birth of all my
> works, from the tenth of August, 1925, memorable day of the
> discovery of *frottage*. (B, 9)

In this way, Ernst specified not just the potentially momentary
nature of *frottage* and collage but also how the viewer might relate to
them. In the process, *frottage* became a defining principle of identity
itself. As Ernst suggests in the final passage of "Beyond Painting":

> When one brings two distant realities together on an appar-
> ently antipathetic plane (that which in simple language is
> called "collage") an exchange of energy transpires, provoked
> by this very meeting. This exchange, which might be a broad
> flowing stream or a shattering stroke of lightning and thunder,
> I am tempted to consider the equivalent of that which, in clas-
> sical philosophy, is called identity. I conclude, in transposing
> the thought of André Breton, that identity will be convulsive
> or it will not exist. (19)

In the Surrealist revision, identity arose from the intersection of
two realities. Ernst expanded this conception by specifying that
this identity emerges from the excess energy generated by that ex-

change. Ernst's Kelvinesque statement circularly privileged collage as the emblem of this form of identity. Collage "forces" the moment of inspiration by rendering it artificially; it manipulates the production of momentary identity first in the act that generates the collage and second in the convulsive identity potentially produced by that collage for the viewer or artist.

Yet even as they enforce this convulsive identity, collage and *frottage* are doomed to remain static. The film theory of Sergei Eisenstein exploited for the mobile form of cinema these same conceptions: the moment of collision generates excess energy and this potentially wasted space can then form the basis of the viewer's experience. In Eisenstein's writings, the governing question became, If momentary intersections produce meaning, where does that meaning occur? And how does it occur, since a film, unlike a collage or photograph, does not allow us to frame each moment? Eisenstein proposed to resolve this dilemma, as a practical problem of film spectatorship, with a mode of momentary activity he called vertical montage. Through vertical montage, the viewer can appropriate momentary constellations of meaning as anchors in the film's drifting mobility. Eisenstein's theory ultimately suggested that cinema reflected the loss of presence by destabilizing a fixed center and by replacing it with a spectatorial drift that exploited putative moments as both the result of the collisions of montage and the sites of "vertical" meaning.

Eisenstein's conception of montage began from the presumption that the single shot forms the building block of cinema: "The shot," he wrote, "is by no means an element of montage. The shot is a montage cell." [19] Yet cinema impels these shot-cells into movement. For Eisenstein, this momentum occurs as the by-product of the violent collisions between each shot and the shot that follows it. "By what, then, is montage characterized and, consequently, its cell— the shot? By collision. By the conflict of two pieces in opposition to each other. By conflict. By collision" (37). Momentary collisions generate the fuel that powers film's forward force. "If montage is to be compared with something," Eisenstein indicated in this same essay, "then a phalanx of montage pieces, of shots, should be compared to the series of explosions of an internal combustion engine, driving forward its automobile or tractor: for, similarly, the dynamics of montage serve as impulses driving forward the total film" (38).

Eisenstein insisted that each collision dialectically produces a third quality, unique to its combination of elements: "Two film pieces of any kind, placed together, inevitably combine into a new concept, a new quality, arising out of that juxtaposition."[20] Eisenstein found the model of this dialectical moment in the Japanese ideogram, which brings together two concepts so as to create a third, different concept.

> The point is that the copulation (perhaps we had better say, the combination) of two hieroglyphs of the simplest series is to be regarded not as their sum, but as their product, i.e., as a value of another dimension, another degree. . . . For example: the picture for water and the picture of an eye signifies "to weep"; the picture of an ear near the drawing of a door = "to listen"; . . . But this is—montage! Yes. It is exactly what we do in the cinema, combining shots that are depictive, single in meaning, neutral in content—into intellectual contexts and series.[21]

Yet this ontological conception could generate meaning only in its ability to engage a spectator. In developing his view of spectatorship from the 1920s through the 1930s, Eisenstein altered his conception of this spectator's momentary experience. In his essay "Eisenstein's Epistemological Shift," David Bordwell argues that Eisenstein's theory of montage changed emphasis around 1929.[22] In the 1920s, Bordwell suggests, Eisenstein emphasized montage as conflict, defining it as the "collision of independent shots— shots even opposite to one another."[23] Shots create meaning from their aggressive confrontation with each other. After 1929, however, Eisenstein moved toward a new model of fusion and cooperation. "The parts of the art work," Bordwell writes, "will be arranged not to collide but to commingle; the goal is not friction but fusion. . . . From now on, montage is harmony and unity" (41).

As in Eisenstein's general theory of montage, the relation between spectator and film changed in this period from aggressive confrontation to participation and collaboration. On the field of spectatorship as much as on that of montage, "the parts of the art work will be arranged not to collide but to commingle." In his early writings, Eisenstein theorized spectatorship in the behaviorist or materialist tradition associated with the experiments of Pavlov. The juxtapositions of montage evoke involuntary physiological responses from the viewer, felt as shocks or jolts. "When the soldiers' boots continue to march downward with a relentless stride," indicated Eisenstein of his film *Battleship Potemkin,* the spectator "involuntarily shrinks back. And seeing the baby carriage of the crazed mother roll down upon the pier he convulsively grips his chair."[24]

As Eisenstein's concept of montage changed, his vision of spectatorship continued to emphasize its momentary nature. But as the film was reconceived from conflict to cooperation, the viewer's momentary experience evolved from the film's aggressive manipulation of response to the viewer's individual appropriation of momentary configurations of meaning. Eisenstein, like Ernst, was interested in how viewers could actually compose meaning from the formal principle of montage. He began this explication by situating film form's spatial nature. Each film sequence, he wrote, is composed of a "simultaneous advance of a multiple series of lines, each maintaining an independent compositional course and each contributing to the total compositional course of the sequence" (FS, 75). Sequences are built from layers of horizontal strata, each "line" representing one aspect. In an example from his own *Old and New,* Eisenstein enumerated such "lines" as the "line of heat, increasing from shot to shot" and the "line of changing close-ups, mounting in plastic intensity" and the "line of mounting ecstasy, shown through the dramatic content of the close-ups" (FS, 75).

These lines "run through and bind together the entire sequence of shots" (FS, 75), but they do not do so monologically. They create relationships among themselves as they progress, systemic relationships that Eisenstein compared to the "vertical structure" of classical music. "Everyone is familiar with the appearance of an orchestral score," he wrote.

> There are several staffs, each containing the part for one instrument or a group of like instruments. Each part is developed

horizontally. But the vertical structure plays no less important a role, interrelating as it does all the elements of the orchestra within each given unit of time. Through the progression of the *vertical* line, pervading the entire orchestra, and interwoven horizontally, the intricate harmonic musical movement of the whole orchestra moves forward. (FS, 74)

The film's horizontal lines move implacably forward but produce meaning only through their dialogue with one another, their systemic relationships. These relationships, for Eisenstein, occur along a vertical axis: at any moment of the film, we could cut downward through the textual layers, as if in archaeological cross section, and discover each line's current position. The film's elements produce meaning through their vertical relations as they progress horizontally; at any point, the horizontal lines engender vertical relations among themselves. No one shot, in other words, is fully present to itself at any one time. This is the level at which Eisenstein's conception of montage dovetails with the vision of lost presence expanded from modernity by Derrida: "The movement of signification," as Derrida has written, "is possible only if each so-called 'present' element, each element appearing on the scene of presence, is related to something other than itself, thereby keeping within itself the mark of the past element, and already letting itself be vitiated by the mark of its relation to the future element."[25] This "economy of traces" describes the nature of Eisensteinian spectatorship, in which "the value of a montage-piece was gauged, not by one feature alone, but always by the whole series of features, before its place in the sequence could be fixed" (FS, 76). The place, the presence, the sited identity of a montage-piece can be determined only by the traces of its relations to the other elements of the system. "This interweaving," as Derrida would put it, "results in each 'element' . . . being constituted on the basis of the trace within it of the other elements in the chain or system."[26]

In Eisenstein's montage system, the viewer's mercurial drift will be regulated on the basis of that form of the montage moment that Eisenstein figured as vertical. Each fleeting moment of the film acquires meaning only through each viewer's vertical taxonomy of the "lines" that pertain to that moment. This concept deployed film's momentary nature as a structure to channel formally and explain discursively the differences in reading between one viewer and another. Where eleven years earlier Eisenstein had written of "that guiding-shot which immediately 'christens' the whole sequence in one 'direction' or another," he now proposed no such signpost to lead the way through the thickets. Eisenstein's earlier view had relied on the Formalist concept of the "dominant," as defined by Formalist critic Yuri Tynyanov: "A system does not mean coexistence of components on the basis of equality; it presupposes the pre-eminence of one group of elements and the resulting deformation of other elements."[27] Yet eleven years after both he and Tynyanov pursued this principle of "preeminence," Eisenstein proposed precisely the "coexistence of components on the basis of equality": "Shot is linked to shot not merely through one indication . . . but through a simultaneous advance of a multiple series of lines, each maintaining an independent compositional course and each contributing to the total compositional course of the sequence" (FS, 75). He not only renounced a dominant center ("not merely through one indication") but repeated the negation by formulating a new systematics: the lines do not bounce off a central tone but instead maintain a "coexistence . . . on the basis of equality," a systematic plurality in which each line maintains "an independent compositional course" and therefore contributes to the sequence's "composite sensation" (FS, 77).

In this polyphonic system, the viewer's responses will not simply reiterate the dominant. Rather, they will form momentary clusters of meaning that anchor the film as it moves continuously forward. The spectator's manufacture of shifting and interrelating "centers" through the course of one viewing, and then potentially through successive viewings, indicates that the film does not present to all spectators at all times an unvarying center or dominant that can be simply unburied. Instead of a dominant that exerts a totalizing influence through the whole film, each vertical arrangement becomes a temporary hierarchy that reacts to the film's horizontal elements. Abandoning the need for a dominating center, Eisenstein seems to revel in the liberation occasioned by "the composite sensation of all the pieces as a whole" (FS, 77), their frictions, reverberations, and tensions free of thematic "domination." The textual system becomes an analogue of the social revolution toward which Eisenstein's ideas were always aimed, as the aesthetic journey from hierarchical dominance to plural liberation mirrors the Soviet Union's shift to communism.

As in Ernst's conceptions of self-distance, Eisenstein's montage moment also provided a fleeting meeting place to yoke together analogically the director's activity and the viewer's experience. This possibility allowed Eisenstein to revise his earlier stimulus/response model of spectatorship, in which "the work of art . . . is above all a tractor reploughing the spectator's psyche,"[28] without rejecting it entirely. When Eisenstein wrote in 1940 that a "work of art, understood dynamically, is just this process of arranging images in the feelings and mind of the spectator" (FS, 17), he retained the director's invasive primacy while adding the concept of process, citing Marx's principle, "Not only the result, but the road to it also, is a part of truth" (FS, 32). Both director and viewer, he now suggested, proceed along the same lines of creation:

> The strength of montage resides in this, that it includes in the creative process the emotions and mind of the spectator. The spectator is compelled to proceed along that selfsame creative road that the author traveled in creating the image. The spectator not only sees the represented elements of the finished work, but also experiences the dynamic process of the emergence and assembly of the image just as it was experienced by the author. . . . In fact, every spectator, in correspondence with his individuality, in his own way and out of his own experience . . . creates an image in accordance with the representational guidance suggested by the author, leading him to understanding and experience of the author's theme. This is the same image that was planned and created by the author, but this image is at the same time created also by the spectator himself. (FS, 32–33)

The contrast in positions could not be more abrupt: once a field to be plowed, the spectator now sits in the tractor. The viewer joins the director in the journey down "that selfsame creative road." The spectator's "individuality," the "warp and weft of his associations," prevents the director from programing a Pavlovian stimulus as if addressing dogs. Director and viewer are conjoined in a process rather than antipodally implicated in a result. The viewer participates in the film by momentarily reexperiencing the creative process that initiated the work. The film's relation to its future viewers is bound up with an invocation of its past production, and this tension between past and future is held in check by the momentary configurations of meaning that situate the viewer's activity as they structure the film's continuity.

This momentary structure reconceived film's iteration along lines of creativity also imagined by Heidegger: "To originate something by a leap, to bring something into being from out of its essential source in a founding leap—this is what the word 'origin' (*Ursprung*, literally, primal leap) means."[29] In this process of cocreation, the film destabilizes a fixed origin. It originates in its creation but cannot continue until "this image is . . . created also by the spectator." The film can exist only through the viewer's act of creation and therefore does not originate simply in its production or simply in its spectatorship but in their momentary configuration, a dialogue between past and present figured spatially as vertical and temporally as an ephemeral present. Production and spectatorship become equally implicated in textual origin; both activities form a source "from which and by which" the film, in Heidegger's terms, "is what it is and as it is" (149). If the "origin of something is the source of its essence" (149), at neither pole is this essence simply, fully present.

In this way, Eisenstein inserted spectatorship's drifting logic into the kind of ontological system in which, as in Derrida's model of context, "there are only contexts without any center of absolute anchoring." The sign, in Derrida's words, "is therefore a mark which remains, which is not exhausted in the present of its inscription, and which can give rise to an iteration both in the absence of and beyond the presence of the empirically determined subject who, in a given context, has emitted or produced it."[30] As Eisenstein indicated, the sign that began in a moment of originary inscription does not simply spin off into the future but is reevoked in a specifically configured later moment that (re)appropriates it. This moment regulates wandering drift as it forms a way station on the road to political change. The momentary interchange between film and viewer opens up the space that Ross Chambers, in literary criticism, has figured as "room for maneuver" between the position offered to the reader by the text and the reader's ongoing lived experience. In this space of negotiation, text and reader both need and change each other: "The text's 'difference' . . . is mediated by reading, the reader's 'difference' from self is mediated by text; the relation of text to reader—another relation of 'difference' or mutual otherness—is mediated by discourse itself." [31]

As the text projects its possibilities onto the field of the reader, so too the reader, in internalizing those possibilities, can refigure himself or herself along a horizon of transformation and metamorphosis. The reader appropriates "room for maneuver"—potentially lost, empty, wasted space—as the site of negotiated change and difference. Wasted space gets turned to use not just as an abstract make-work project but as a mode of personal and political evolution. As Chambers writes, "It is because discourse is systematic that it produces 'room for maneuver,' and reading is the name of that maneuvering, out of which change can result" (18). In opening up vertical montage as the momentary means of this individualized reading, Eisenstein deployed the wasted spaces of encounter and collision not just for the experiential drift of spectatorship but for the dialectical possibility of political change as a consequence of textual experience. Rather than drift in the passive sense, the viewer could appropriate constellations of meaning and aim them toward a utopian horizon of personal and social transformation.

• • •

Monet sat in front of that cathedral and painted it over and over again.

He sat on a boat and painted the sunrise over and over again.

Trying to seize the fleeting moment will make you crazy.

Degas gave up and started taking photographs.

The thick paint, the light and brushstrokes—they all just underline the futility of trying to capture that moment.

Impressionism is a shrine to the lost moment.

The lost moment as a fetish object.

In Impressionist painting, the possibility of a stable moment finally and firmly died.

Do you think they sensed it?

Do you think that's why they were so palpably desperate, frantically trying to capture each moment?

Hungrily trying to sop up every moment.

Greedy, arrogant, desperate.

•   •   •

The Museum of Copies.

You have to admit it's a brilliant idea.

Forget about aura, about how the painting has a unique history and it's a single object and so forth.

The Museum of Copies sees through that.

Each painting is a subset of the hunger to make the present present.

Come back little present.

What's the difference between a painting that re-presents a painting the painter saw and a painting that re-presents something else the painter saw?

If the painting's just a copy, it loses its aura.

But every painting's just a copy.

That's why the Museum of Copies is so brilliant.

It calls aura's bluff.

•   •   •

I took Benjamin to the Museum of Copies and tried to make him see this.

It confirmed my worst suspicions.

He's secretly in love with presence.

He's covertly a sensualist.

He kept trying to tell me that the paintings still have an aura, less than "real" paintings, but still more than photographs or other mass-circulated things.

And it hit me so clearly.

Aura's just a form of presence.

Aura's a way to talk about presence after you've acknowledged that nothing can be present.

Benjamin's just shifting presence around.

He's setting up an intellectual shell game to hide the recuperation of presence.

You can't be too hard on him.

You can see his desire.

Without presence, life is boring.

· · ·

S I X

The End of Pleasure

If the "moment" is a category of experience constructed by contrasts among perceived states of feeling, then the sublime moment,
which manifests a peak of intense feeling, represents the emblematic form of momentary experience. The experience of sublime
feeling has traditionally been figured as a sensation so profound
that it seems to transport the person who feels it to another realm.[1]
Narrating an 1847 trip to the island of Belle-Ile, Flaubert provided
a vivid description of this transportational sublime: "Our spirit,"
he wrote, "revolved in the profusion of these splendors, we drank
them in with our eyes; we flared our nostrils to them, we opened
our ears to them. . . . By force of penetrating us, entering us, we
became nature too, we felt her gaining on us and we experienced
an immeasurable joy; we would have wanted to become lost in her,
be taken by her, or carry her off in us."[2] Although Flaubert's experience was clearly durational, it also relied on such momentary
figures as penetration, entrance, being taken, and being carried off.
If pleasure was "gaining on us," that running-up process invoked
the gradual buildup to a peak moment in which sublime feeling
overtakes its subject. The clearing of the senses described in the

first sentence creates an open field on which the subject becomes available for the instant of sharp sensation that defines the sublime.

From its earliest expression by Longinus in the first century, the sublime had been defined as a moment in which the subject is suddenly arrested by a feeling so intense that it can only wane in the moments that follow.[3] Sublime sensation is by definition momentary because it is both unanticipated and fleeting. The moment of sublime feeling exemplifies evanescent sensation, marked off by contrast with the less intense feelings immediately before and after it. But the sublime was not fully reformulated as momentary and sensual until the writings of Walter Pater in the early 1870s. Pater's primary statements on individual sensational response were contained in the preface and the infamous conclusion to his book first titled *Studies in the History of the Renaissance* in 1873 and then republished in 1877, with the conclusion excised, under the title *The Renaissance: Studies in Art and Poetry,* the title it retained in the third edition, with a revised conclusion, in 1888. As this checkered history suggests, Pater's conclusion was in its time a polarizing and controversial document that, in the delicate words of Pater's latter-day editor Harold Bloom, "cost Pater considerable preferment at Oxford."[4] In his introduction to Pater's work, Bloom gleefully quotes a scornful paraphrase of Pater's aesthetic by "this very minor Wordsworth"—William's grandnephew John—who after the first edition summed up Pater's position as, in part, "the only thing worth living for is momentary enjoyment." Pater's dry response to this charge indicates that it is not really wrong: "I wish they would not call me a hedonist. It gives such a wrong impression to those who do not know Greek."

Pater basically did believe, although it oversimplifies his stance, that "the only thing worth living for is momentary enjoyment." As he wrote in one of the conclusion's aphorisms, "Not the fruit of experience, but experience itself, is the end" (60). Pater had no interest in pragmatic, goal-oriented results, in concrete data accrued through experience. Rather, he advocated a sensual immersion in the present tense of experience: "Art comes to you," he concluded the conclusion, "professing frankly to give nothing but the highest quality to your moments as they pass, and simply for those moments' sake" (62). For Pater, we seize value from our lives by inhabiting as many sensual moments as we can. As he urged in one of his better-known exhortations, "To burn always with this hard, gemlike flame, to maintain this ecstasy, is success in life" (60). You can imagine how and why this startlingly unguarded definition of "success in life" as the preservation of "ecstasy" alienated conservative and religious minds at Oxford, leading Pater, in hasty overreaction, to suppress it entirely.

Yet to emphasize this hedonism underestimates Pater's aesthetic, which in these two short essays built momentary sensual immersion into an epistemological and critical framework. In Pater's view, we can know the world only through our momentary sensual responses, a necessity acted out in aesthetic appreciation. The terms of Pater's analysis consistently shift between critical evaluation and epistemological generalization. I can begin to evaluate a work of art only if I have first assessed its sensual and emotional impact, not abstractly but tangibly. "In aesthetic criticism," Pater wrote in the preface, "the first step towards seeing one's object as it really is, is to know one's own impression as it really is, to discriminate it, to realise it distinctly. . . . What is this song or picture . . . to *me*? What effect does it really produce on me? Does it give me pleasure? and if so, what sort or degree of pleasure?" (17–18).

For Pater, the individual's subjective responses to the work of art provide criticism's raw material: "The answers to these questions," he suggested after the passage above, "are the original facts with which the aesthetic critic has to do; and, as in the study of light, of morals, of number, one must realise such primary data for oneself, or not at all" (18). Pater slyly and polemically gave ballast to the airiness of his subjectivist model by allying it to the same "original facts" and "primary data" one encounters "in the study of light, of morals, of number." This association was licensed by the philosophical movement to which it might seem most opposed: the Positivism that held conceptual sway before and during the period in which Pater wrote.[5] Positivism stressed the centrality of individual observation, of the impressions received by the individual off the surface of the world. Under this influence, Pater argued that the individual's subjective response to the work of art constitutes a "fact" of the natural world as much as light for science and numbers for math. While Positivism led in one direction to scientific repeatability, it also contained this emphasis on individual observation that veered in the opposite direction from objective experimentation.

Pater's formulation undermined Positivism's aspirations to concrete repeatability by suggesting the contradiction at Positivism's heart: the emphasis on individual observation leads more plausibly to a doctrine of sensual subjectivity than to one of objective observation. His dictum "Not the fruit of experience, but experience itself, is the end" pointedly aimed toward Positivism's desire to harness experience for verifiable, scientistic ends. The statement expressed the extent to which Pater's treatise represented not a mindlessly hedonistic call to sensation but a carefully crafted polemic that sought to rescue momentary experience from the dry practicality to which Positivism had consigned it.

Pater developed his aesthetic by exploiting this paradoxical insistence on the empirical validity of subjective feeling. In the paragraph of the preface already discussed, he first suggested a traditional, commonsense defense of empirical experience over abstract theorizing: "He who experiences these impressions strongly . . . has no need to trouble himself with the abstract question what beauty is in itself, or what its exact relation to truth or experience—metaphysical questions, as unprofitable as metaphysical questions elsewhere. He may pass them all by as being, answerable or not, of no interest to him" (18). This rejection of the metaphysical in favor of the concrete experience of impressions rejected Positivism on its own terms. Pater dismissed the "metaphysical" as offhandedly as did the most hardheaded Positivist, concerned only with the immediate data of practical life. Yet he did so in the service of those qualities of emotion and pleasure that might seem most typically irrational.

The next sentence makes even clearer that for Pater the experiences of pleasure and sensation form data as tangible as any other facts of the natural world: "The aesthetic critic, then, regards all the objects with which he has to do, all works of art, and the fairer forms of nature and human life, as powers or forces producing pleasurable sensations, each of a more or less peculiar and unique kind" (18). In this radical statement, Pater elucidated his means of adapting Positivist methodology to his subjectivist aesthetic. What matters are not the objective objects but the "pleasurable sensations" they produce. It is not objects that are "peculiar and unique," thereby eliciting the critic's investigation, but the sensations of pleasure they generate; artworks "are valuable . . . as we say, in speaking of an herb, a wine, a gem; for the property each has of affecting one with a special, a unique, impression of pleasure" (18). These sensations then become the object of the aesthetic critic's activity, which is based in the Humean presumption that the momentary impression mediates between the subject and the world: "The function of the aesthetic critic," Pater specified, "is to distinguish, analyse, and separate from its adjuncts, the virtue by which a picture, a landscape, a fair personality in life or in a book, produces this special impression of beauty or pleasure, to indicate what the source of that impression is, and under what conditions it is experienced" (18). Pater carefully included in his sphere of interest both the nature of the object and the experience of the subject. The bridge between these two areas would be the fleeting sensual impression.

Through this insistence on ephemeral response, Pater opened the door for the moment's pedagogical possibilities. Sensual attention to the surface of the world became a way to know it more deeply and feel it more keenly. "Philosophical theories or ideas, as points of view, instruments of criticism," Pater wrote, "may help us to gather up what might otherwise pass unregarded by us" (61). The ephemeral moment of sensual impression becomes through retrospection a vehicle of defamiliarization, opening our eyes to the "splendour of our experience" to which daily life otherwise habituates us.

• • •

The show I like is *Wheel of Fortune*.

Have you seen this show?

People spin a wheel and solve puzzles with missing letters.

Like H–PP– B–RTHDA–.

You have to buy letters to fill in the puzzle.

Each puzzle is its own mystery, its own narrative.

You follow it from beginning to middle to end.

It's about filling empty spaces, and it always ends happily.

•   •   •

It's not just the game shows I like but the awards shows.

They're both about loss—loss as a spectacle.

They seem to be about winning but they're really about losing.

We don't want to see people win; we want to see them lose.

On the awards shows, watch the other four faces when someone wins: loss frozen like a fossil into that instant.

You can't get it back, but it's fixed there forever.

These shows become tapestries of losses.

They're the material of the inexorable loss of time, moment by moment, inscribed into re-presentation.

•   •   •

People think I change channels mindlessly, but it's not true.

I just can't get enough.

They think I'm catatonic.

They think I sit here numbed-out by the shows.

But it's the opposite: I can't get over it.

There's so much to see, so much to experience, so many new things to learn.

This has to be the greatest invention in history, and I can't tell you how glad I am that I got to see it.

There's always something happening, all the time.

There are always dozens and dozens of different things happening, all the time, all at the same time.

How can you choose among them?

Why would you ever sleep? There's so much to take in, and so little time, and as soon as you settle on one thing you're missing so many other things.

It's a huge machinery of pleasure.

It's so much better than life.

•   •   •

People say all this time watching TV distracts you from leading your real life.

But I think it's the other way around.

Everyday life is so boring, you're scavenging for whatever moments of pleasure you can find.

Life distracts you from television.

What you call everyday life is already distracted.

You are already distracted from your actual life, which is going on behind you. I see that now.

So what's the difference?

It's all the same; it's all representation.

My experience of myself is no different from my experience of TV shows, which is no different from my experience of you.

If you look at it that way, you have to admit TV's your best option.

With TV shows, you get the most pleasure per moment.

Hunt around, track down every moment of pleasure, maximize each instant.

Try not to waste a minute.

•   •   •

TV channel-hopping eliminates the empty spaces; it shears off the waste.

Movies have all this dead space.

So does life.

TV does too, but if I get the zapping just right, I can suture them out. I can make TV one big montage of peak moments.

It's a game I play with myself, to get as close to this as possible. How fast can I zap away from the dead spots?

Can I get away so quickly that I beat the empty moment?

Get up there ahead of it?

It could happen, and I keep trying.

It looks like I'm spellbound, but it's the reverse.

I'm trying to seize control. I'm obsessed.

•   •   •

Photogénie

In his concept of *photogénie* in 1920s France, Jean Epstein envisioned the momentary sublime as the unique element of the new art of cinema. "One has hardly begun to perceive," Epstein insisted, "that an unexpected art has produced itself. Totally new. We must realize what that represents."[6] Epstein wanted to derive the specificity of this new modern art, and he found it in the sublime instants he called *photogénie*. "It is surprising enough to say," he stated with typical irony in a 1923 lecture, "but literature must first of all be literary; theater, theatrical; painting, pictoral; and cinema, cinematic. . . . Cinema must seek step by step to become, finally, uniquely cinematic, that is, to use only photogenic elements. *Photogénie* is the purest expression of cinema" (137–38). For Epstein, this specificity arose from what he called those "photogenic elements" or, as he put it, *photogénie*. "With the notion of *photogénie*," he proposed in a 1924 lecture, "the idea of cinema-art is born. For how better to define the indefinable *photogénie* than to say: *photogénie* is for cinema what color is for painting, volume for sculpture—the specific element of that art" (145).

What, then, is this great discovery, this one element that defines "the essence of cinema"? Herein lies the paradox. Epstein's conceptual leap was to ally film to irrationality, indefinability, instability—qualities that a film theorist cannot specify, quantify, or describe. Epstein set out to define cinema, but the definition was indefinable. Cinema's essence relies on its elusiveness, its always-moving-away. For Epstein, the essence of cinema occurred not in its narrative capacities but in the moments of powerful feeling that certain images provide. *Photogénie* marks the place of these uncanny effects. "One racks one's brains in wanting to define it," he wrote of *photogénie*. "Face of beauty, it's a taste of things. I recognize it like a musical phrase" (91). Moreover, *photogénie* is by definition fleeting: "*Photogénie* is a value on the order of the second. If it is long, I don't find continuous pleasure in it. . . . Until now I have never seen pure *photogénie* lasting an entire minute" (94).

Despite this insistence that cinema's definition lies in its indefinability, Epstein endeavored to clarify, without muddying the term's intrinsic opacity, what he meant by *photogénie*. In a 1923 discussion, he mocked the effort to quantify the essence of cinema: "Undergoing, one day, the interview of a journalist, I had to answer several questions destined, I believe, . . . to pierce this mystery of the identity of cinema" (119). Epstein's strategically jocular tone only partially masks his genuine aversion to the effort "to pierce this mystery." Throughout this misbegotten interview, he takes pleasure in continuing to mystify that identity. To make a short story shorter, the journalist keeps asking Epstein whether certain qualities do or do not represent the essence of cinema. Epstein portrays himself as baffled or amused by these questions and at the end admits, "We therefore return again and always to the question: 'What are the aspects of things, beings, and souls that are photogenic, aspects to which the cinematic art has the duty to limit itself?'" (120). Epstein answers this question in three terse sentences: "The photogenic aspect is a component of space-time variables. This is an important formula. If you want a more concrete translation, here it is: an aspect is photogenic if it displaces itself and varies simultaneously in space and time" (120).

Epstein's language here retained its characteristically sly edge. His "concrete" position is anything but concrete, as it embodies the generative paradox of his idea of *photogénie*, which defines the essence of cinema as indefinable. Pressed for "concrete" specification, Epstein first employed bluster, bafflement, and irony, until he found his best revenge in a grudging "definition" that was only about movement and change. Epstein's definition of *photogénie* deconstructs itself: claiming concreteness, it reconfirms *photogénie's* elusiveness. *Photogénie*, Epstein insisted through this definition, is defined as change and variation. Its essence lies in its inability to be pinned down to the graspability of a concrete definition. It is dis-placed. Epstein expressed his distaste for the concreteness even of language in a typical passage from a 1924 lecture: "Around what

one wants to say words skid like wet bars of soap," he said, destabilizing the very form of the lecture in which he expressed these
thoughts. He continued:

> This evening a friend who wanted to explain everything to
> me too exactly suddenly raised his arms twice and said no
> more. . . . And when the scholar labors to use words with pre-
> cision, I no longer believe. . . . There are twelve good words
> for each thing, and at least twelve things for each word. . . .
> On the line of communication the static of unexpected feel-
> ings interrupts us. Everything remains to be said, and we give
> it up, exhausted. (146)

The disruption of a linear message by "the static of unexpected
feelings" describes *photogénie*'s relation to narrative cinema. Yet
this phrase also gestured toward *photogénie*'s evocation of a deeper,
supernatural reality. "No texts. The true film does without them,"
Epstein tersely stated, slyly adding, in denigration of D. W. Griffith,
"*Broken Blossoms* could have done so" (93). He followed this dictum
with: "But supernatural. The cinema is supernatural in its essence,"
as he also wrote that "cinema is psychic" (91). These assertions cor-
relate with the prevailing mysticism (or mystification) of Epstein's
view of cinema. But this notion of a psychic or supernatural quality
also touches on Epstein's conception of the cinematic moment as a
consequence of two of cinema's defining elements, mechanical reproduction and the deployment of space and time.

"What is *photogénie?*" Epstein again asked in a 1923 lecture. But
he gave an answer somewhat different from his emphasis elsewhere
on just space and time. "I would call photogenic any aspect of
things, beings, and souls that augments its moral quality by cinematic reproduction. And any aspect that is not improved by cinematic reproduction is not photogenic, does not form part of the
cinematic art" (137). Epstein suggested that the moment of contact
between mechanical reproduction and the world brings something
out of people and objects that we would not otherwise see. It en-
hances them. "The click of a shutter makes a *photogénie* which did
not exist before it" (91).

In part, this moment is an effect of defamiliarization. By reperceiving the world in its photographic and cinematic reproductions, one finds that "well-springs of life gush out of corners that one believed sterile and explored" (92). But Epstein's view of defamiliarization has an uncanny cast. He felt not only that we experience things freshly through the cinema but also that the moment of contact with the film lens elicits from people and objects a "soul" that we would not otherwise perceive. Things have a "personality" that *photogénie* brings out of them: "All the aspects of the world, elected to the world by cinema, are elected only on the condition that they have their own personality. This is the second specification that we can now add to the rules of *photogénie*. I therefore propose that we say: only the mobile and personal aspects of things, beings, and souls can be photogenic, that is, acquire a superior moral value by cinematic reproduction" (140).

Here as elsewhere, Epstein casually included "souls" among "things and beings." The notion that souls have as tangible an existence as people and objects constituted a key polemical point for Epstein, whose seemingly offhand, mystical style always proves more canny and strategic than it might at first appear. But how, exactly, do these souls manifest themselves? Paradoxically, through mechanical reproduction, the new technology that might seem most destined to destroy the soul's fragile aura. In the re-production of the physical universe, something new emerges. "Our eye, without very long practice, cannot discover it directly. A lens centers it, drains it, and distills *photogénie* between its focal planes" (91). Because, in the mechanically reproduced image, we resee something familiar, the reproduction allows us to focus on new qualities, eliciting something that our habituated perceptions could not discover. "On screen," he writes, "we re-see what the cinema has already seen once" (91). The viewer appropriates as a supernatural defamiliarization the breach opened up between the object and its photogenic reproduction. The object's supernatural aura can be construed only in the gap that separates the on-screen object from the real-world object, and this difference can be forged only by the viewer and on the basis of that interval.

By becoming part of the photogenic, the on-screen object differs from what it was before; the new context makes it a new object, even if it can be traced referentially to the concrete object that existed in front of the camera. Cinema resides in re-presentation, a notion that Epstein associated with a literally super-natural power. *Photogénie* embodies repetition, yet the repetition is ineffably different. This is the photogenic effect. In the reiteration of the object, its soul and essence float to the surface and accost our jaded perceptions. Because we see in a new frame things familiar to us, we see their soul, essence, or personality. This defamiliarization explains Epstein's attribution to cinema of "psychic" tendencies: the cinema is psychic in that it can see into the essences of people and objects, and it is supernatural in the literal sense that it surpasses the natural enclosures that surround "things and beings."

For another crucial aspect of his theory, the conception of space and time, Epstein again reached for a psychic image, polemically proposing that "the gift of clairvoyants is to conceive simultaneously space and time" (239). Here we return to Epstein's definition of *photogénie* as an element that "varies simultaneously in space and time." The photogenic defines cinema as an art that forms a nexus of space and time. For Epstein, the cinema is emblematically modern in this union of space and time, and cinema's ability to move and change across space and time defines its essence. "The lamentable poverty of scenarios," he suggested, "arises in the first place from the failure to appreciate this primordial rule: there are no inactive feelings, that is, not displacing themselves in space; there are no invariable feelings, that is, not displacing themselves in time" (121). This is why, with his typically careful wording, he emphasized that "only the mobile . . . aspects of things, beings, and souls can be photogenic." Cinema is above all about mobility—"*Photogénie* . . . does not let in stasis" (94)—and mobility crosses both space and time.

When Epstein considered time in relation to the present tense, he moved toward a more specific conception of the viewer's experience. "Man's physiological inability to master the notion of space-time," he wrote, "is not limited to a metaphysical deficiency. One could maintain that the human mind's powerlessness to escape the present, which holds an exclusive grip on its consciousness, is the cause of most accidents. . . . much would be avoided if we were capable of immediately seizing the world as a continuation and not as an instant" (239). For Epstein, the present moment is a conceptual convenience that, in practice, no one can experience. "There is no real present," he proposed in one of his most philosophically serious passages,

> today is a yesterday, perhaps old, that brings in the back door a tomorrow, perhaps far-away. The present is an uneasy convention. In the midst of time, it is an exception to time. It escapes the chronometer. You look at your watch; the present strictly speaking is already no longer there, and strictly speaking it is there again, it will always be there from one midnight to the next. I think therefore I was. The future I bursts into past I; the present is only this instantaneous and incessant molt. The present is only a meeting. Cinema is the only art that can represent this present as it is. (179–80)

Like Bergson, Epstein presents the present as something that can exist only as the place where past and future collide. Cinema marks the emergence of an art form that can reflect this temporal reality. Moreover, Epstein's vacated present opens a space for the viewer's activity. The viewer's experience becomes the only present tense available to the film. The film must predicate its unstoppable movement on the viewer as a floating present tense, the pivot of the action. This viewer is not a present tense in a stable, idealist sense. Rather, in conceiving the viewer's activity as "a continuation and not as an instant," Epstein envisions spectatorship as a continuing, mobile activity that does not halt inside a discrete pit stop called the present.

> The animation and the confluence of these forms produce themselves neither on the film strip nor in the lens but only in the individual himself. Discontinuity becomes continuity only after penetrating the spectator. It is a purely interior phenomenon. Outside the subject who looks, there is no movement, no flux, no life in the always fixed mosaics of light and shadow that the screen presents. Within, there is an impression that, like all the others given by the senses, is an interpretation of the object—in other words, an illusion, a phantom. (261)

A film becomes like any other sensation received and interpreted by the body's sense organs. This formulation in itself embodies spectatorship as experiential, intimately intertwined with the viewer as a living body that negotiates not just film viewing but life in general. Above all, Epstein emphasized that the film does not exist outside the viewer's invisible interior activity. Hurtling from past to future, the film is present only in the viewer's activity; it assumes presence only in that interval. Spectatorship thus becomes a creative appropriation of the film; filtered through the mind, the viewer's reception of the film becomes as much an imaginative construction as the mind's other "illusions." Comprehension has no tangible, corporeal presence and thus becomes, like the film itself, "a phantom."

● ● ●

People think I'm so traumatized by the loss of pleasure that I can only sit
    and stare at the television.
They're missing the point.
It's such a relief to get away from the burden of pleasure.
I wrecked my life for pleasure.
People hated my book, I almost lost my job, I had to keep suppressing
    my ideas.
All for pleasure.
It wasn't worth it.
It's a phantom.
A chimera.
I see that now.
Now I can't invest any moment with pleasure.
I've liberated myself from the need to give every moment a meaning.
Pleasure takes so much energy.

● ● ●

What do you do for fun, people ask me.
I object to the premise of the question.
Fun is a shallow concept, trivial, insubstantial.

A trick, a hoax, a practical joke, says the dictionary.

What's the opposite of fun? Seriousness, soberness, work.

Nothing's wrong with those things. Fun is on the wrong side of that equation.

•   •   •

I took pleasure very seriously.

I saw pleasure as the aim of life, but if fun is the aim of your life, you couldn't be a very serious person.

What's the opposite of pleasure? Pain. No one wants that.

Pleasure has a purpose. It keeps away the pain.

And bliss is something else entirely. Bliss always implied to me a vacuity, a smiling spaciness: blissed-out, as they say.

I'm convinced—well, I'm determined—that it shouldn't be impossible to feel some of these things. Even here.

This is my quest.

I don't see how you can live without pleasure.

People think I'm just sitting there, zoning out in front of the television, feeling sorry for myself, mourning my lost life.

I'm not wasting time.

Time is wasted for me. Wasting time would be a waste of time.

I'm thinking, I'm brooding, I'm hatching a plan.

How do you make pleasure?

•   •   •

Not the fruit of experience, but experience itself, is the end.

I got into so much trouble for saying this.

I was trying to get people to pay attention to their sensations.

I was so frustrated by empiricism, by positivism, as if all that mattered were results, as if everything you did and felt fed into a machine of right answers.

I wanted people to be sensual, responsive.

It made me seem like a hedonist, and I don't think that was right, because it implies someone who's frivolous, wallowing in self-absorbed pleasure, and I don't see myself that way at all.

A hedonist indulges in bliss, but bliss, as I've said, was never my inclination.

I wasn't necessarily talking about pleasure at all.

I just wanted people to be intimate with their own experience, to listen to it.

Now I see what raw experience is like.

It's not so much fun.

• • •

This is why I'm fascinated by television.

It's like raw experience but better: so much going on, more than you can assimilate, each moment going by with so much lost, so much unseen, ungrasped.

You feel the loss, but you feel the pleasure too.

It's a trade-off, except for me, it's better than a trade-off, because it's the only kind of pleasure I get.

Television has become my salvation.

It's the opposite of pain.

I get so frustrated by people who don't realize that if you lose continuous moments, you're going to lose emotions too.

It only makes sense, and I've gotten used to it. You can't make senses into meaning if there's no space for it to happen, no next moment to collapse into.

But I miss it, and television gives me a parallel track, a way to beat the discontinuous moment at its own game and on its own (as if I had a choice) terms.

If I'm not allowed to grab pleasure in my own experience, I'll snatch it out of TV experience.

That's why I have to concentrate and stay still and quiet and sit there as long as I can.

Don't tell anyone.

. . .

As I see it, fun depends on action, bliss needs continuity, but pleasure is a
    seizure, it's fragmentary and partial, it's selfish, it's appropriated inside
    empty and jagged fissures.
Jumping around the channels, aimlessly spinning through them, every-
    thing equal, stopping at nothing, flattening everything out—this is
    what a lot of people do, what people call zapping or channel hopping.
What's the point of that?
It just repeats the flattening out, the boredom, the loss.
Everything's the same. Nothing matters.
You've already got that in your life. Why reiterate it?
That's my definition of fun.
It's a leaping, a lunging, a puppy hopping on everything, dumb, indis-
    criminate.
Jumping all over the channels like a slobbering puppy.

. . .

My problem always was, I could never feel just pleasure.
I wanted to isolate each moment of pleasure so that I could set it apart
    from the other things I had to feel to feel pleasure, to know it as plea-
    sure.
Does it give me pleasure? and if so, what sort or degree of pleasure?
But there is no way to ascertain this without experiencing so many things
    that are not pleasure.
So that you know the difference.
So that you recognize pleasure when you see it.
Pleasure is only difference.
It's only the name for something you feel that has another kind of energy
    from something else you feel.
It's only produced in the space that separates it from other feelings.
I hated having to feel those other things.
I wanted to refine everything down to just pleasure.

Get as close to this as possible.

Like eating the cashews out of the mixed nuts.

$$\bullet \quad \bullet \quad \bullet$$

I used to think it was a waste of time to feel anything other than pleasure.

What made me think pleasure was so special.

What made me think pleasure was immune to waste.

I was trying to use pleasure as a wall against the battering tide of loss and waste.

As if pleasure could mitigate the waste of every moment.

As if pleasure weren't part of it, could be kept separate from it.

Everyone's looking for something to save them.

Pleasure was my religion, my astrology.

I thought I was too good for faith, I thought I didn't need that kind of crutch.

But we're all lusting for some kind of faith, something to give it a meaning, a purpose, beyond the pointlessness, the ephemerality, the evaporation.

I thought pleasure was the answer.

I didn't see that I'd fallen into the trap.

$$\bullet \quad \bullet \quad \bullet$$

I wanted to shear off everything but pleasure, get life down to as many moments of pleasure as possible.

But pleasure needs that waste, it thrives on it, it grows on the ground of that waste.

Pleasure is only difference, and pleasure makes no difference.

It's the name for a chimera, and the chimera's already gone.

It's not going to stop every moment from going away. It's not going to stop the end from coming.

In the face of all that loss and pointlessness, at least you can enjoy yourself.

That's what I thought, at least.

But it doesn't help.

It doesn't change anything.

It only makes it worse.

The higher you go, the lower you fall.

• • •

Pleasure's the wrong horse to ride if you're looking to redeem time.

Because it makes you feel that ephemerality.

It makes you hungry for more.

You can't stop at just one moment.

If you're bored or unhappy or miserable or mourning or in grief, you can't wait for those moments to pass away; ephemerality is your best friend.

Pleasure's a horrible drug that makes you want more and more the more you have. You want to hold on to each moment, you want each moment to last as long as it can, you want more and more moments in series. And you can't have these things. And you didn't care before you got hooked on pleasure.

That's pleasure's revenge. You use it, you throw it away, but it gets you back.

• • •

So you see I was wrong, because I didn't want to acknowledge that nothing comes for free.

Art comes to you professing frankly to give nothing but the highest quality to your moments as they pass, and simply for those moments' sake.

But it's never simply for those moments' sake.

Those moments are predicated on the other moments, the valleys around the pleasures.

How could I not see this; it seems so obvious.

Strong emotions are a hedge against the passing of the present, but pleasure's the only one that makes it worse.

• • •

What's more useless than pleasure?

Pleasure patrols the borders of use; it defines the excess around the useful, the practical.

Like everything, it goes away. But what does it accomplish while it's here?
Nothing.

You can see I've turned against pleasure.

What did it get me?

What did it do for me?

All it ever did was go away.

All it ever did was wane and leave me wanting more.

Needing more.

Pleasure is pure waste.

There's just this huge collection of sensations, and each one goes away like the others, and one of them is called pleasure, and it makes no difference.

Pleasure is just a way to feel something else.

•   •   •

S E V E N

A Horizontal Line

• • •

Benjamin understood loss.

He felt it, in his soul, and he knew what was coming.

That's why he gave up, killed himself before he would have been saved.

He grasped how, moment by moment, everything gets lost, and everything gets lost over and over again, new moment by new moment by
past moment by new moment.

The past pops up like a flash of lightning and fades away again.

And that form of that past is never coming back.

Grab it while you can.

• • •

He gave up hope that he would be saved.

That's what people say.

I think it's more complicated.

I think he understood that it didn't matter.

That everything is lost.

And he couldn't take the loss anymore.

Too much loss, too literal and palpable.

His worst fears confirmed.

Philosophy made flesh and packed off to die.

· · ·

So he took refuge.

In the idea of the Messiah and in the idea that you could sense the present.

Which are the same idea.

In the Now of recognizability, something appears on the scene of presence.

We sense it, feel it, recognize it as a presence.

Then it's gone.

Of course it was never there in the first place, but Benjamin needed something to hang on to, some shred of hope when he had torn everything else apart.

Believing you might be able to sense the present is a leap of faith, like believing the Messiah will come.

· · ·

The painter Agnes Martin said in an interview:

"One time, I was coming out of the mountains, and having painted the mountains, I came out on this plain, and I thought, Ah! What a relief! . . . I thought, This is for me! The expansiveness of it. I sort of surrendered. This plain . . . it was just like a straight line. It was a horizontal line."

This is how it feels to be here. To surrender to the empty moment. Stop trying to outrun it. Breathe. Relax. Drift.

Martin, of course, was talking about death.

My grandmother stood on the street, said "Isn't it a beautiful day," and
   died.
She died in that instant.
In the moment of death, the body rests because it has caught up to itself.

Notes

One. Drift

1 Alfred Wegener, *The Origin of Continents and Oceans,* trans. John Biram (New York: Dover, 1966), p. 17.

2 Marshall Berman, *All That Is Solid Melts into Air: The Experience of Modernity* (New York: Simon and Schuster, 1981).

3 Ross Chambers, *Room for Maneuver: Reading (the) Oppositional (in) Narrative* (Chicago: University of Chicago Press, 1991).

4 All translations are from *Chekhov: The Major Plays,* trans. Ann Dunnigan (New York: Signet, 1964).

5 My translations from Marcel Proust, *Du côté de chez Swann* (Paris: Gallimard, 1919).

6 Richard E. Goodkin, *Around Proust* (Princeton: Princeton University Press, 1991), p. 86.

7 Georg Simmel, "The Metropolis and Mental Life," in *The Sociology of Georg Simmel,* ed. Kurt Wolff, trans. H. H. Gerth (New York: Free Press, 1950), p. 410.

8 Sir William Thomson, "On a Universal Tendency in Nature to the Dissipation of Mechanical Energy," in *Mathematical and Physical Papers* (Cambridge: Cambridge University Press, 1882), 1:511–14. Further page references will be given parenthetically in the text and will be to volume 1.

9 See especially Ilya Prigogine and Isabelle Stengers, *Order out of Chaos* (New York: Bantam, 1984). See also N. Katherine Hayles, ed., *Chaos and Order: Complex Dynamics in Literature and Science* (Chicago: University of Chicago Press, 1991), particularly Hayles's useful introduction.

10 Edward Bellamy, *Looking Backward: 2000–1887* (Boston: Houghton Mifflin, 1887), pp. 229–30.

11 Cecelia Tichi, *Shifting Gears: Technology, Literature, Culture in Modernist America* (Chapel Hill: University of North Carolina Press, 1987), p. 57. Chapter 2 provides a detailed discussion of modern conceptions of waste and efficiency, especially in relation to industry and technology.

12 Roland Barthes, *The Pleasure of the Text*, trans. Richard Miller (New York: Hill and Wang, 1975), pp. 18–19. Further page references will be given parenthetically in the text.

13 Jürgen Habermas, "Modernity versus Postmodernity," trans. Selya Ben-Habib, *New German Critique* 22 (winter 1981): 5.

14 Edmund Husserl, *The Phenomenology of Internal Time-Consciousness*, ed. Martin Heidegger, trans. James Churchill (Bloomington: Indiana University Press, 1964). Further page references will be given parenthetically in the text.

15 Martin Heidegger, *Being and Time*, trans. John Macquarrie and Edward Robinson (New York: Harper and Row, 1962), p. 388. Further page references will be given parenthetically in the text.

Two. The Present Moment

1 Virginia Woolf, "The Moment: Summer's Night," in *"The Moment" and Other Essays* (New York: Harcourt Brace Jovanovich, 1948), pp. 3–8. Further page references will be given parenthetically in the text.

2 William James, *Principles of Psychology* (New York: Holt, 1890), p. 680.

3 Heidegger, *Being and Time*, p. 387.

4 James, *Principles of Psychology*, p. 613. On Wundt's experiments, see Jonathan Crary, "Unbinding Vision: Manet and the Attentive Observer in the Late Nineteenth Century," in *Cinema and the Invention of Modern Life*, ed. Leo Charney and Vanessa R. Schwartz (Berkeley: University of California Press, 1995), pp. 49–51.

5 Husserl, *Phenomenology of Internal Time-Consciousness*.

6 Gotthold Lessing, *Laocoön: An Essay on the Limits of Painting and Poetry*, trans. Edward Allen McCormick (New York: Bobbs-Merrill, 1962), p. 19. Further page references will be given parenthetically in the text.

7 Auguste Rodin, *Art: Conversations with Paul Gsell*, trans. Jacques de Caso and Patricia B. Sanders (Berkeley: University of California Press, 1984), pp. 31, 32.

8 On the intersections between Cubism and film, see Standish Lawder, *The Cubist Cinema* (New York: New York University Press, 1975).

9 Alfred Barr, ed., *Picasso: Fifty Years of His Art* (New York: Museum of Modern Art, 1946), p. 271.

10 André Salmon, *La jeune peinture française* (Paris: Messein, 1912), p. 51; my translation.

11 Albert Gleizes and Jean Metzinger, "On Cubism," in *Modern Artists on Art*, ed. Robert Herbert (Englewood Cliffs, N.J.: Prentice-Hall, 1964), p. 15.

12 Guillaume Apollinaire, *The Cubist Painters: Aesthetic Meditations*, trans. Lionel Abel (New York: Wittenborn, Schultz, 1949), pp. 10, 14, 10.

13 Barr, *Picasso*, p. 272.

14 Victor Shklovsky, "Art as Technique," in *Russian Formalist Criticism: Four Essays*,

trans. Lee T. Lemon and Marion J. Reis (Lincoln: University of Nebraska Press, 1965), p. 12. On Russian Formalism see Victor Erlich, *Russian Formalism: History—Doctrine*, 3d ed. (New Haven: Yale University Press, 1981).

15 Sigmund Freud, "The 'Uncanny,'" in *Collected Papers*, vol. 4, trans. Joan Riviere (New York: Basic, 1959). Page references will be given parenthetically in the text.

16 As Robin Wood has argued, this kind of disruption has been the generative theme of horror films. See "Introduction to the American Horror Film," in *Hollywood from Vietnam to Reagan* (New York: Columbia University Press, 1988).

17 Antonin Artaud, "Witchcraft and the Cinema," in *Collected Works*, vol. 3, trans. Alastair Hamilton (London: Calder and Boyars, 1972), p. 66.

18 Germaine Dulac, "The Essence of the Cinema: The Visual Idea," trans. Robert Lamberton, in *The Avant-Garde Film: A Reader of Theory and Criticism*, ed. P. Adams Sitney (New York: New York University Press, 1978), p. 39.

19 Walter Benjamin, "The Work of Art in the Age of Mechanical Reproduction," in *Illuminations*, ed. Hannah Arendt, trans. Harry Zohn (New York: Schocken, 1969), p. 236.

20 Richard Abel, "The Contribution of the French Literary Avant-Garde to Film Theory and Criticism (1907–1924)," *Cinema Journal* 14, 3 (spring 1975): 28.

21 Tom Gunning, "The Cinema of Attraction: Early Film, Its Spectator, and the Avant-Garde," *Wide Angle* 8, 3/4 (1986); and Gunning, "An Aesthetic of Astonishment: Early Film and the (In)Credulous Spectator," *Art and Text* 34 (spring 1989).

22 Tom Gunning, "'Now You See It, Now You Don't': The Temporality of the Cinema of Attractions," *Velvet Light Trap* 32 (fall 1993): 6–7.

23 Sergei Eisenstein, "Montage of Attractions," in *The Film Sense*, trans. and ed. Jay Leyda (New York: Harcourt Brace, 1942), pp. 230–31.

24 Jacques Aumont, *Montage Eisenstein*, trans. Lee Hildreth, Constance Penley, and Andrew Ross (Bloomington: Indiana University Press/London: British Film Institute, 1987), p. 42.

25 My citations from the Arcades Project will be to the partial translation by Leigh Hafrey and Richard Sieburth of Walter Benjamin, "N [Re the Theory of Knowledge, Theory of Progress]," in *Benjamin: Philosophy, Aesthetics, History*, ed. Gary Smith (Chicago: University of Chicago Press, 1989). See also Susan Buck-Morss, *The Dialectics of Seeing: Walter Benjamin and the Arcades Project* (Cambridge: MIT Press, 1989); and Miriam Hansen, "Benjamin, Cinema, and Experience: 'The Blue Flower in the Land of Technology,'" *New German Critique* 40 (winter 1987).

26 Walter Benjamin, "On Some Motifs in Baudelaire," in Arendt, *Illuminations*, p. 156.

27 Ibid., pp. 163, 194.

28 Smith, *Benjamin*, p. 38.

29 Richard Sieburth, "Benjamin the Scrivener," in Smith, *Benjamin*, pp. 26–27.

30 Hafrey and Sieburth's "exhibit" translates the German *zeigen*, which, as Sieburth notes in "Benjamin the Scrivener," more broadly connotes "to show, to exhibit, to indicate, to say by pointing, to silently name" (22).

31 Arendt, introduction to *Illuminations*, p. 47.

32 Walter Benjamin, "Theses on the Philosophy of History," in Arendt, *Illumina-tions*, p. 255.

33 My discussion of the "Now of recognizability" is indebted to Margaret Cohen, *Profane Illumination: Walter Benjamin and the Paris of Surrealist Revolution* (Berkeley: University of California Press, 1993).

34 Sieburth, "Benjamin the Scrivener," p. 24.

35 Benjamin, "Motifs in Baudelaire," p. 163.

36 See the more extended discussion of the distinction between *Erlebnis* and *Er-fahrung*, both German terms for "experience," in Cohen, *Profane Illumination*, esp. pp. 180–92, 205–8. There is a also a useful explanation of this issue in the translators' preface to the second, revised edition of Hans-Georg Gadamer, *Truth and Method* (New York: Crossroad, 1989), pp. xiii–xiv.

37 Crary, "Unbinding Vision," p. 50. Also see Roger Smith, *Inhibition* (Berkeley: University of California Press, 1992).

38 *Stanislavsky on the Art of the Stage,* trans. David Magarshack (London: Faber and Faber, 1950), p. 141. Further page references will be given parenthetically in the text.

39 See Ernst, "How One Forces Inspiration," in *Max Ernst: Beyond Painting,* trans. Dorothea Tanning (New York: Wittenborn, Schultz, 1948).

40 Ferdinand de Saussure, *Course in General Linguistics,* ed. Charles Bally and Albert Sechehaye, with Albert Riedlinger, and trans. Wade Baskin (New York: McGraw Hill, 1966), pp. 111–12. Further page references will be given paren-thetically in the text.

41 Jacques Derrida, *"Différance,"* in *Margins of Philosophy,* trans. Alan Bass (Chi-cago: University of Chicago Press, 1982), p. 11.

42 M. H. Abrams, "The Deconstructive Angel," *Critical Inquiry* 3, 3 (spring 1977): 431.

Three. Peaks and Valleys

1 Henri Delaborde, "Le Musée des Copies," *Revue des deux mondes,* 1 May 1873, pp. 213–16; my translation.

2 On this culture, see Christoph Asendorf, *Batteries of Life: On the History of Things and Their Perception in Modernity,* trans. Don Reneau (Berkeley: Univer-sity of California Press, 1993).

3 On Impressionist painting and modernity, see esp. T. J. Clark, *The Painting of Modern Life: Paris in the Art of Manet and His Followers* (New York: Knopf, 1985); and Robert Herbert, *Impressionism: Art, Leisure, and Parisian Society* (New Haven: Yale University Press, 1988).

4 Vanessa R. Schwartz, "Cinematic Spectatorship before the Apparatus: The Pub-lic Taste for Reality in *Fin-de-Siècle* Paris," in Charney and Schwartz, *Cinema and the Invention of Modern Life.* Page references will be given parenthetically in the text. My understanding of turn-of-the-century modernity is indebted to Schwartz's dissertation, *The Public Taste for Reality: Early Mass Culture in Fin-de-Siècle Paris* (University of California at Berkeley, 1993), now revised and expanded as *Spectacular Realities: Early Mass Culture in Fin-de-Siècle Paris* (Berkeley: University of California Press, 1998).

5 Simmel, "Metropolis and Mental Life," p. 410.

6 On this point see Stephen Kern, *The Culture of Time and Space, 1880–1918* (Cambridge: Harvard University Press, 1983).

7 Crary, "Unbinding Vision," pp. 50–51.

8 Anne Friedberg, *Window Shopping: Cinema and the Postmodern* (Berkeley: University of California Press, 1993), p. 3. See also Giuliana Bruno, *Streetwalking on a Ruined Map: Cultural Theory and the City Films of Elvira Notari* (Princeton: Princeton University Press, 1993); Priscilla Parkhust Ferguson, *Paris as Revolution: Writing the Nineteenth-Century City* (Berkeley: University of California Press, 1994), esp. chap. 3; and Janet Wolff, "The Invisible *Flâneuse*," in *Feminine Sentences* (Berkeley: University of California Press, 1990).

9 David Nasaw, *Going Out: The Rise and Fall of Public Amusements* (New York: Basic, 1993), provides a useful overview of such American diversions as the amusement park, the baseball game, the city, and ultimately the cinema.

10 See John Culhane, *The American Circus* (New York: Holt, 1990).

11 Morris Werner, *Barnum* (New York: Harcourt Brace, 1923), p. 312.

12 Albert-Emile Sorel cited and translated in Charles Rearick, *Pleasures of the Belle Epoque: Entertainment and Festivity in Turn-of-the-Century France* (New Haven: Yale University Press, 1985), p. 149.

13 Kathy Peiss, *Cheap Amusements: Working Women and Leisure in Turn-of-the-Century New York* (Philadelphia: Temple University Press, 1986).

14 In addition to Peiss, see John Kasson, *Amusing the Million: Coney Island at the Turn of the Century* (New York: Hill and Wang, 1978); and Lauren Rabinovitz, "Temptations of Pleasure: Nickelodeons, Amusement Parks, and the Sights of Female Sexuality," *Camera Obscura* 23 (May 1990).

15 Brooks McNamara, "Come On Over: The Rise and Fall of the American Amusement Park," *Theatre Crafts* 11, 4 (September 1977): 85.

16 Kasson, *Amusing the Million*, p. 82.

17 More than ten years before Coney Island, roller coasters existed in Paris as free-standing *montagnes russes* surrounded by cafés and pleasure gardens. See Rearick, *Pleasures of the Belle Epoque*, esp. p. 75.

18 Among the extensive literature on sports and modernity, see esp. John Betts, *American Sporting Heritage: 1850–1950* (Reading, Mass.: Addison-Wesley, 1974); Allen Guttmann, *From Ritual to Record: The Nature of Modern Sports* (New York: Columbia University Press, 1978); Stephen Reiss, *City Games: The Evolution of American Urban Society and the Rise of Sports* (Urbana: University of Illinois Press, 1989); Dale Somers, *The Rise of Sports in New Orleans, 1850–1900* (Baton Rouge: Louisiana State University Press, 1972); and Stephen Reiss, ed., *The American Sporting Experience: A Historical Anthology of Sport in America* (New York: Leisure Press, 1984).

19 Professional football began in 1895 but did not catch on until the 1920s and 1930s. The best overview of this development is Douglas Noverr and Lawrence Ziewacz, eds., *The Games They Played: Sports in American History, 1865–1980* (Chicago: Nelson-Hall, 1983), chap. 5.

20 Patrice Petro, *Joyless Streets: Women and Melodramatic Representation in Weimar Germany* (Princeton: Princeton University Press, 1989), p. 59. See also Siegfried

Kracauer, *The Mass Ornament,* ed. and trans. Thomas Y. Levin (Cambridge: Harvard University Press, 1995).

21 Frederick Winslow Taylor, *The Principles of Scientific Management* (1911; reprint, New York: Norton, 1967). See also Taylor's authorized biography by Frank Barkley Copley, *Frederick W. Taylor: Father of Scientific Management* (New York: Taylor Society, 1923); and on Taylor's influence, Martha Banta, *Taylored Lives: Narrative Productions in the Age of Taylor, Veblen, and Ford* (Chicago: University of Chicago Press, 1993), esp. chap. 1.

22 See David Bordwell, Janet Staiger, and Kristin Thompson, *The Classical Hollywood Cinema: Film Style and Mode of Production to 1960* (New York: Columbia University Press, 1986).

23 Raymond Bellour, "Hitchcock, the Enunciator," trans. Bertrand Augst and Hilary Radner, *Camera Obscura* 2 (fall 1977): 83.

24 Stephen Heath, "Film and System: Terms of Analysis, Part II," *Screen* 16, 2 (summer 1975): 99. On film and excess, see also Kristin Thompson, "The Concept of Cinematic Excess," in *Narrative, Apparatus, Ideology,* ed. Philip Rosen (New York: Columbia University Press, 1986); and Leo Charney, "Historical Excess: *Johnny Guitar's* Containment," *Cinema Journal* 29, 4 (summer 1990).

25 Roland Barthes, *Camera Lucida: Reflections on Photography,* trans. Richard Howard (New York: Hill and Wang, 1981), p. 49.

26 Siegfried Kracauer, *Theory of Film: The Redemption of Physical Reality* (New York: Oxford University Press, 1960), p. 165.

27 On the evolution of parallel editing, see Eileen Bowser, *The Transformation of Cinema, 1907-1915* (New York: Scribner's, 1990), chap. 4; Tom Gunning, *D. W. Griffith and the Origins of American Narrative Film* (Urbana: University of Illinois Press, 1991); Gunning, "Weaving a Narrative: Style and Economic Background in Griffith's Biograph Films," *Quarterly Review of Film Studies* 6, 1 (winter 1981); and Bordwell, Staiger, and Thompson, *The Classical Hollywood Cinema,* pp. 48–49, 210–12.

28 See the overview of this development in Bordwell, Staiger, and Thompson, *The Classical Hollywood Cinema,* pp. 198–203.

29 Scott Higgins has examined how this fragmentation dominated the films of the so-called transitional period between 1907 and 1917. See his "Motivation and Spatial Fragmentation in the Cinema of Narrative Integration" (paper delivered at the Society for Cinema Studies conference, March 1994).

30 Joel Silver quoted in Mark Singer, "The Joel Silver Show," *New Yorker,* 21 March 1994, p. 128.

Five. Boredom

1 Mary Ann Caws, *The Poetry of Dada and Surrealism* (Princeton: Princeton University Press, 1970), pp. 14–15.

2 Comte de Lautréamont, *Les Chants de Maldoror,* trans. Guy Wernham (New York: New Directions, 1965), p. 263.

3 André Breton, *Mad Love,* trans. Mary Ann Caws (Lincoln: University of Nebraska Press, 1987), pp. 99, 17–19. Breton drew his awareness of astrology from the French culture of the 1930s and 1940s, in which astrology enjoyed unusual

cultural currency. These horoscopes featured not the twelve sun-sign predictions familiar from contemporary horoscopes but a more general account of upcoming planetary activity. Breton's conception of astrological encounter reflected this emphasis. See Claude Fischler, Philippe Defrance, and Lena Petrossian, eds., *La croyance astrologique moderne* (Paris: Editions l'Age d'Homme, 1981), esp. Fischler, "L'astrologie de masse," pp. 43–63.

4   André Breton, *Manifestoes of Surrealism,* trans. Richard Seaver and Helen R. Lane (Ann Arbor: University of Michigan Press, 1969), pp. 123–24.

5   André Breton, *Signe ascendant* (Paris: Gallimard, 1949), p. 7; my translations.

6   André Breton, *Communicating Vessels,* trans. Mary Ann Caws and Geoffrey Harris (Lincoln: University of Nebraska Press, 1990), p. 65.

7   Pierre Reverdy, "L'image," *Nord-Sud* 13 (March 1918); my translations. Reverdy repeated his ideas in *Le gant de crin* (1927; reprint, Paris: Flammarion, 1968), a collection of aphorisms about art.

8   My overview of the Surrealists' interest in film can be supplemented by Richard Abel's seminal article "The Contribution of the French Literary Avant-Garde to Film Theory and Criticism (1907–1924)" and by Paul Hammond, ed., *The Shadow and Its Shadow: Surrealist Writing on the Cinema,* rev. ed. (Edinburgh: Polygon, 1991). On Surrealist film, see Linda Williams, *Figures of Desire: A Theory and Analysis of Surrealist Film* (Berkeley: University of California Press, 1981); and Rudolf E. Kuenzli, ed., *Dada and Surrealist Film* (New York: Willis, Locker and Owens, 1987).

9   Artaud, "Witchcraft and the Cinema," p. 66. Further page references are given parenthetically in the text.

10 Ado Kyrou, *Le surréalisme au cinéma* (Paris: Arcanes, 1953), pp. 9, 11; my translation. Marguerite Bonnet makes similar points in "L'aube de surréalisme et le cinéma: Attente et rencontres," *Etudes cinématographiques* 38/39 (spring 1965). In this same special issue on Surrealism, see also J. H. Matthews, "Du cinéma comme langage Surréaliste."

11 Apollinaire cited and translated in Abel, p. 27.

12 Jean Epstein, *Ecrits sur le cinéma, 1921–1953,* vol. 1, *1921–1947* (Paris: Seghers, 1974), p. 91; my translation. Further references will be given parenthetically in the text; all are my translation.

13 Dulac, "Essence of the Cinema," p. 39; further page references will be given parenthetically in the text. For more on Dulac, see Sandy Flitterman-Lewis, *To Desire Differently: Feminism and the French Cinema* (Urbana: University of Illinois Press, 1990), chaps. 2–4.

14 *Kino-Eye: The Writings of Dziga Vertov,* ed. Annette Michelson, trans. Kevin O'Brien (Berkeley: University of California Press, 1984), p. 18. Further page references will be given parenthetically in the text.

15 Germaine Dulac, "From 'Visual and Anti-Visual Films,' " trans. Robert Lamberton, in *Avant-Garde Film,* ed. Sitney, pp. 31–34. Further page references will be given parenthetically in the text.

16 On the connection between Eisensteinian montage and the Surrealist encounter, see Michel Beaujour, "Qu'est-ce que 'Nadja'?" *La nouvelle revue française* 172 (April 1967): esp. 782.

17 I will cite "How One Forces Inspiration" and "Beyond Painting" (B) from the

translations by Dorothea Tanning in *Max Ernst: Beyond Painting* (New York: Wittenborn, Schultz, 1948). Page references will be given parenthetically in the text.

18 I have modified the Tanning translation here and in the following passage, both of which inexplicably miss the point by translating the French "assiste" (attend) as "assist."

19 Sergei Eisenstein, "The Cinematographic Principle and the Ideogram" (1929), in *Film Form: Essays in Film Theory*, ed. and trans. Jay Leyda (New York: Harcourt Brace, 1949), p. 37.

20 Eisenstein, *Film Sense* (FS), p. 4. Further page references to FS will be given parenthetically in the text.

21 Eisenstein, "Cinematographic Principle and the Ideogram," pp. 29–30.

22 David Bordwell, "Eisenstein's Epistemological Shift," *Screen* 15, 4 (winter 1974/75).

23 Sergei Eisenstein, "A Dialectic Approach to Film Form" (1931), in *Film Form*, p. 49.

24 "Eisenstein's Technique," *New York Times*, 25 February 1927, sec. 8, p. 5.

25 Derrida, *"Différance,"* in *Margins of Philosophy*, p. 13.

26 Jacques Derrida, *Positions*, trans. Alan Bass (Chicago: University of Chicago Press, 1981), p. 26.

27 Yuri Tynyanov cited and translated in Erlich, *Russian Formalism*, p. 199.

28 Sergei Eisenstein, "On the Question of a Materialist Approach to Form," trans. Roberta Reeder, in Sitney, *Avant-Garde Film*, p. 18.

29 Martin Heidegger, "The Origin of the Work of Art," in *Basic Writings*, ed. David Farrell Krell (New York: Harper and Row, 1977), p. 186. Further page references will be given parenthetically in the text.

30 Jacques Derrida, "Signature Event Context," in *Margins of Philosophy*, p. 317.

31 Chambers, *Room for Maneuver*, pp. 17–18.

Six. The End of Pleasure

1 On the premodern Romantic sublime, see Immanuel Kant, *Critique of Judgement*, trans. James Creed Meredith (Oxford: Clarendon, 1952); "The Sublime and the Beautiful: Reconsiderations," *New Literary History* 16, 2 (winter 1985); and Thomas Weiskel, *The Romantic Sublime: Studies in the Structure and Psychology of Transcendence* (Baltimore: Johns Hopkins University Press, 1976).

2 Flaubert is cited and translated in Steven Z. Levine, "Seascapes of the Sublime: Vernet, Monet, and the Oceanic Feeling," *New Literary History* 16, 2 (winter 1985): 377.

3 On the history of the sublime, see, in addition to the works cited in n. 1 to this chapter, Samuel H. Monk, *The Sublime* (Ann Arbor: University of Michigan Press, 1960); and Peter de Bolla, *The Discourse of the Sublime* (Oxford: Basil Blackwell, 1989).

4 *Selected Writings of Walter Pater*, ed. Harold Bloom (New York: Columbia University Press, 1974), p. xxi. All references to Pater will be to this edition and will be given parenthetically in the text.

5 On Positivism, see, among others, Emile Littré, *La science au point de vue phi-*

losophique (Paris: Hachette, 1876); and D. G. Charlton, *Positivist Thought in France during the Second Empire, 1852–70* (London: Oxford University Press, 1959).

6   Epstein, *Ecrits sur le cinéma,* 1:145; my translation. All future citations to Epstein will be given parenthetically in the text from this volume and will be my translations. Selections from some of Epstein's most important articles and lectures appear in English translation in *Afterimage,* no. 10; *October,* no. 3; and Sitney, *Avant-Garde Film.* On French Impressionist theory, see Richard Abel, ed., *French Film Theory and Criticism: A History/Anthology, 1907–1939* (Princeton: Princeton University Press, 1988); David Bordwell, *French Impressionist Cinema: Film Culture, Film Theory, and Film Style* (New York: Arno, 1980); and Stuart Liebman, "French Film Theory, 1910–1921," *Quarterly Review of Film Studies* 8, 1 (winter 1983).

Bibliography

Modernity

Abel, Richard, ed. *French Film Theory and Criticism: A History/Anthology, 1907–1959*. Princeton: Princeton University Press, 1988.

Apollinaire, Guillaume. *The Cubist Painters: Aesthetic Meditations*. Trans. Lionel Abel. New York: Wittenborn, Schultz, 1949.

Artaud, Antonin. "Witchcraft and the Cinema." In *Collected Works*. Vol. 3. Trans. Alastair Hamilton. London: Calder and Boyars, 1972.

Bachelard, Gaston. *La dialectique de la durée*. Paris: Boivin, 1936. Reprint, Paris: Presses universitaires de France, 1972.

―――. *L'intuition de l'instant*. Paris: Gonthier, 1932.

Barr, Alfred, ed. *Picasso: Fifty Years of His Art*. New York: Museum of Modern Art, 1946.

Bellamy, Edward. *Looking Backward: 2000–1887*. Boston: Houghton Mifflin, 1887.

Benjamin, Walter. "N [Re the Theory of Knowledge, Theory of Progress]." Trans. Leigh Hafrey and Richard Sieburth. In *Benjamin: Philosophy, Aesthetics, History*, ed. Gary Smith. Chicago: University of Chicago Press, 1989.

―――. "The Work of Art in the Age of Mechanical Reproduction." In *Illuminations*, ed. Hannah Arendt and trans. Harry Zohn. New York: Schocken, 1969.

Bergson, Henri. *Creative Evolution*. Trans. Arthur Mitchell. New York: Modern Library, 1944.

―――. *Duration and Simultaneity, with Reference to Einstein's Theory*. Trans. Leon Jacobson. Indianapolis: Bobbs-Merrill, 1965.

―――. *Matter and Memory*. Trans. Nancy Margaret Paul and W. Scott Palmer. New York: Zone, 1988.

Breton, André. *Communicating Vessels.* Trans. Mary Ann Caws and Geoffrey Harris. Lincoln: University of Nebraska Press, 1990.

——. *Mad Love.* Trans. Mary Ann Caws. Lincoln: University of Nebraska Press, 1987.

——. *Manifestoes of Surrealism.* Trans. Richard Seaver and Helen R. Lane. Ann Arbor: University of Michigan Press, 1969.

——. *Signe ascendant.* Paris: Gallimard, 1949.

Chekhov, Anton. *The Major Plays.* Trans. Ann Dunnigan. New York: Signet, 1964.

Copley, Frank Barkley. *Frederick W. Taylor: Father of Scientific Management.* New York: Taylor Society, 1923.

Delaborde, Henri. "Le Musée des Copies." *Revue des deux mondes,* 1 May 1873.

Dulac, Germaine. "The Essence of the Cinema: The Visual Idea." Trans. Robert Lamberton. In *The Avant-Garde Film: A Reader of Theory and Criticism,* ed. P. Adams Sitney. New York: New York University Press, 1978. Originally published in *Les cahiers du mois* 16/17 (1925).

——. "From 'Visual and Anti-Visual Films.'" Trans. Robert Lamberton. In *The Avant-Garde Film: A Reader of Theory and Criticism,* ed. P. Adams Sitney. New York: New York University Press, 1978. Originally published in *Le rouge et le noir,* July 1928.

Eisenstein, Sergei. *Film Form: Essays in Film Theory.* Ed. and trans. Jay Leyda. New York: Harcourt Brace, 1949.

——. *The Film Sense.* Ed. and Trans. Jay Leyda. New York: Harcourt Brace, 1942.

Epstein, Jean. *Ecrits sur le cinéma, 1921–1953.* Paris: Seghers, 1974.

Ernst, Max. *Max Ernst: Beyond Painting.* Trans. Dorothea Tanning. New York: Wittenborn, Schultz, 1948.

Freud, Sigmund. "The 'Uncanny.'" In *Collected Papers.* Vol. 4. Trans. Joan Riviere. New York: Basic, 1959.

Gleizes, Albert, and Jean Metzinger. "On Cubism." In *Modern Artists on Art,* ed. Robert Herbert. Englewood Cliffs, N.J.: Prentice-Hall, 1964.

Hammond, Paul, ed. *The Shadow and Its Shadow: Surrealist Writing on the Cinema.* Rev. ed. Edinburgh: Polygon, 1991.

Heidegger, Martin. *Being and Time.* Trans. John Macquarrie and Edward Robinson. New York: Harper and Row, 1962.

——. "The Origin of the Work of Art." In *Basic Writings,* ed. David Farrell Krell. New York: Harper and Row, 1977.

Husserl, Edmund. *The Phenomenology of Internal Time-Consciousness.* Ed. Martin Heidegger. Trans. James Churchill. Bloomington: Indiana University Press, 1964.

James, William. *Principles of Psychology.* New York: Holt, 1890.

Kracauer, Siegfried. *The Mass Ornament: Weimar Essays.* Ed. and trans. Thomas Y. Levin. Cambridge: Harvard University Press, 1995.

——. *Theory of Film: The Redemption of Physical Reality.* New York: Oxford University Press, 1960.

Lautréamont, Comte de. *Les Chants de Maldoror.* Trans. Guy Wernham. New York: New Directions, 1965.

Littré, Emile. *La science au point de vue philosophique.* Paris: Hachette, 1876.

Muybridge, Eadweard. *Muybridge's Complete Human and Animal Locomotion*. New York: Dover, 1979.

Pater, Walter. *Selected Writings of Walter Pater*. Ed. Harold Bloom. New York: Columbia University Press, 1974.

Proust, Marcel. *Du côté de chez Swann*. Paris: Gallimard, 1919.

Reverdy, Pierre. *Le gant de crin*. 1927. Reprint, Paris: Flammarion, 1968.

———. "L'image." *Nord-Sud* 13 (March 1918).

Rodin, Auguste. *Art: Conversations with Paul Gsell*. Trans. Jacques de Caso and Patricia B. Sanders. Berkeley: University of California Press, 1984.

Salmon, André. *La jeune peinture française*. Paris: Messein, 1912.

Saussure, Ferdinand de. *Course in General Linguistics*. Ed. Charles Bally and Albert Sechehaye, with Albert Riedlinger. Trans. Wade Baskin. New York: McGraw Hill, 1966.

Shklovsky, Victor. "Art as Technique." In *Russian Formalist Criticism: Four Essays*, trans. Lee T. Lemon and Marion J. Reis. Lincoln: University of Nebraska Press, 1965.

Simmel, Georg. "The Metropolis and Mental Life." *The Sociology of Georg Simmel*. Ed. Kurt Wolff. Trans. H. H. Gerth. New York: Free Press, 1950.

Stanislavsky, Konstantin. *Stanislavsky on the Art of the Stage*. Trans. David Magarshack. London: Faber and Faber, 1950.

Taylor, Frederick Winslow. *The Principles of Scientific Management*. 1911. Reprint, New York: Norton, 1967.

Thomson, Sir William. "On a Universal Tendency in Nature to the Dissipation of Mechanical Energy." In *Mathematical and Physical Papers*. Vol. 1. Cambridge: Cambridge University Press, 1882. Originally published in *Proceedings of the Royal Society of Edinburgh*, 19 April 1852.

Vertov, Dziga. *Kino-Eye: The Writings of Dziga Vertov*. Ed. Annette Michelson. Trans. Kevin O'Brien. Berkeley: University of California Press, 1984.

Wegener, Alfred. *The Origin of Continents and Oceans*. Trans. John Biram. New York: Dover, 1966.

Woolf, Virginia. "The Moment: Summer's Night." In *"The Moment" and Other Essays*. New York: Harcourt Brace Jovanovich, 1948.

On and After Modernity

Abel, Richard. "The Contribution of the French Literary Avant-Garde to Film Theory and Criticism (1907–1924)." *Cinema Journal* 14, 3 (spring 1975).

Asendorf, Christoph. *Batteries of Life: On the History of Things and Their Perception in Modernity*. Trans. Don Reneau. Berkeley: University of California Press, 1993.

Aumont, Jacques. *Montage Eisenstein*. Trans. Lee Hildreth, Constance Penley, and Andrew Ross. Bloomington: Indiana University Press/London: British Film Institute, 1987.

Banta, Martha. *Taylored Lives: Narrative Productions in the Age of Taylor, Veblen, and Ford*. Chicago: University of Chicago Press, 1993.

Barthes, Roland. *The Pleasure of the Text*. Trans. Richard Miller. New York: Hill and Wang, 1975.

Beaujour, Michel. "Qu'est-ce que 'Nadja'?" *La nouvelle revue française* 172 (April 1967).

Berman, Marshall. *All That Is Solid Melts into Air: The Experience of Modernity*. New York: Simon and Schuster, 1981.

Betts, John. *American Sporting Heritage: 1850–1950*. Reading, Mass.: Addison-Wesley, 1974.

Bohrer, Karl Heinz. *Suddenness: On the Moment of Aesthetic Appearance*. Trans. Ruth Crowley. New York: Columbia University Press, 1994.

Bolla, Peter de. *The Discourse of the Sublime*. Oxford: Basil Blackwell, 1989.

Bonnet, Marguerite. "L'aube de surréalisme et le cinéma: Attente et rencontres." *Etudes cinématographiques* 38/39 (spring 1965).

Bordwell, David. "Eisenstein's Epistemological Shift." *Screen* 15, 4 (winter 1974/75).

———. *French Impressionist Cinema: Film Culture, Film Theory, and Film Style*. New York: Arno, 1980.

Bordwell, David, Janet Staiger, and Kristin Thompson. *The Classical Hollywood Cinema: Film Style and Mode of Production to 1960*. New York: Columbia University Press, 1986.

Bowser, Eileen. *The Transformation of Cinema, 1907–1915*. New York: Scribner's, 1990.

Braun, Marta. *Picturing Time: The Work of Etienne-Jules Marey (1830–1904)*. Chicago: University of Chicago Press, 1992.

Bruno, Giuliana. *Streetwalking on a Ruined Map: Cultural Theory and the City Films of Elvira Notari*. Princeton: Princeton University Press, 1993.

Buck-Morss, Susan. *The Dialectics of Seeing: Walter Benjamin and the Arcades Project*. Cambridge: MIT Press, 1989.

Caws, Mary Ann. *The Poetry of Dada and Surrealism*. Princeton: Princeton University Press, 1970.

Chambers, Ross. *Room for Maneuver: Reading (the) Oppositional (in) Narrative*. Chicago: University of Chicago Press, 1991.

Charlton, D. G. *Positivist Thought in France during the Second Empire, 1852–70*. London: Oxford University Press, 1959.

Charney, Leo, and Vanessa R. Schwartz, eds. *Cinema and the Invention of Modern Life*. Berkeley: University of California Press, 1995.

Clark, T. J. *The Painting of Modern Life: Paris in the Art of Manet and His Followers*. New York: Knopf, 1985.

Cohen, Margaret. *Profane Illumination: Walter Benjamin and the Paris of Surrealist Revolution*. Berkeley: University of California Press, 1993.

Crary, Jonathan. *Techniques of the Observer: On Vision and Modernity in the Nineteenth Century*. Cambridge: MIT Press, 1990.

Culhane, John. *The American Circus*. New York: Holt, 1990.

Dagognet, François. *Etienne-Jules Marey: La passion de la trace*. Paris: Hazan, 1987.

Deleuze, Gilles. *The Logic of Sense*. Trans. Mark Lester, with Charles Stivale. New York: Columbia University Press, 1990.

Derrida, Jacques. *Margins of Philosophy*. Trans. Alan Bass. Chicago: University of Chicago Press, 1982.

———. "The Double Session." In *Dissemination,* trans. Barbara Johnson. Chicago: University of Chicago Press, 1981.

Erlich, Victor. *Russian Formalism: History—Doctrine*. 3d ed. New Haven: Yale University Press, 1981.

Ferguson, Priscilla Parkhust. *Paris as Revolution: Writing the Nineteenth-Century City*. Berkeley: University of California Press, 1994.

Friedberg, Anne. *Window Shopping: Cinema and the Postmodern*. Berkeley: University of California Press, 1993.

Frisby, David. *Fragments of Modernity: Theories of Modernity in the Work of Simmel, Kracauer, and Benjamin*. Cambridge: MIT Press, 1986.

Goodkin, Richard E. *Around Proust*. Princeton: Princeton University Press, 1991.

Gunning, Tom. "An Aesthetic of Astonishment: Early Film and the (In)Credulous Spectator." *Art and Text* 34 (spring 1989).

———. "The Cinema of Attraction: Early Film, Its Spectator, and the Avant-Garde." *Wide Angle* 8, 3–4 (1986).

———. *D. W. Griffith and the Origins of American Narrative Film*. Urbana: University of Illinois Press, 1991.

———. "'Now You See It, Now You Don't': The Temporality of the Cinema of Attractions." *Velvet Light Trap* 32 (fall 1993).

———. "Weaving a Narrative: Style and Economic Background in Griffith's Biograph Films." *Quarterly Review of Film Studies* 6, 1 (winter 1981).

Guttmann, Allen. *From Ritual to Record: The Nature of Modern Sports*. New York: Columbia University Press, 1978.

Habermas, Jürgen. "Modernity versus Postmodernity." Trans. Selya Ben-Habib. *New German Critique* 22 (winter 1981).

Hansen, Miriam. *Babel and Babylon: Spectatorship in American Silent Film*. Cambridge: Harvard University Press, 1991.

———. "Benjamin, Cinema, and Experience: 'The Blue Flower in the Land of Technology.'" *New German Critique* 40 (winter 1987).

Hayles, N. Katherine, ed. *Chaos and Order: Complex Dynamics in Literature and Science*. Chicago: University of Chicago Press, 1991.

Herbert, Robert. *Impressionism: Art, Leisure, and Parisian Society*. New Haven: Yale University Press, 1988.

Huyssen, Andreas. *After the Great Divide: Modernism, Mass Culture, Postmodernism*. Bloomington: Indiana University Press, 1986.

Kasson, John. *Amusing the Million: Coney Island at the Turn of the Century*. New York: Hill and Wang, 1978.

Kern, Stephen. *The Culture of Time and Space, 1880–1918*. Cambridge: Harvard University Press, 1983.

Kirby, Lynne. *Parallel Tracks: The Railroad and Silent Cinema*. Durham: Duke University Press, 1997.

Kuenzli, Rudolf E., ed. *Dada and Surrealist Film*. New York: Willis, Locker, and Owens, 1987.

Kyrou, Ado. *Le surréalisme au cinéma*. Paris: Arcanes, 1953.

Lawder, Standish. *The Cubist Cinema*. New York: New York University Press, 1975.

Liebman, Stuart. "French Film Theory, 1910–1921." *Quarterly Review of Film Studies* 8, 1 (winter 1983).

Lightman, Alan. *Einstein's Dreams*. New York: Pantheon, 1993.

Martin, Agnes. *Writings*. Ed. Dieter Schwarz. Stuttgart: Cantz, 1991.

Matthews, J. H. "Du cinéma comme langage Surréaliste." *Etudes cinématographiques* 38/39 (spring 1965).

McNamara, Brooks. "Come On Over: The Rise and Fall of the American Amusement Park." *Theatre Crafts* 11, 4 (September 1977).

———. "The Scenography of Popular Entertainment." *Drama Review* 18, 1 (March 1974).

Monk, Samuel H. *The Sublime*. 1935. Reprint, Ann Arbor: University of Michigan Press, 1960.

Musser, Charles. *The Emergence of Cinema: The American Screen to 1907*. New York: Scribner's, 1990.

Nasaw, David. *Going Out: The Rise and Fall of Public Amusements*. New York: Basic, 1993.

Noverr, Douglas, and Lawrence Ziewacz, eds. *The Games They Played: Sports in American History, 1865–1980*. Chicago: Nelson-Hall, 1983.

Orvell, Miles. *The Real Thing: Imitation and Authenticity in American Culture, 1880–1940*. Chapel Hill: University of North Carolina Press, 1989.

Peiss, Kathy. *Cheap Amusements: Working Women and Leisure in Turn-of-the-Century New York*. Philadelphia: Temple University Press, 1986.

Petro, Patrice. *Joyless Streets: Women and Melodramatic Representation in Weimar Germany*. Princeton: Princeton University Press, 1989.

Prigogine, Ilya, and Isabelle Stengers. *Order out of Chaos*. New York: Bantam, 1984.

Rabinovitz, Lauren. "Temptations of Pleasure: Nickelodeons, Amusement Parks, and the Sights of Female Sexuality." *Camera Obscura* 23 (May 1990).

Rearick, Charles. *Pleasures of the Belle Epoque: Entertainment and Festivity in Turn-of-the-Century France*. New Haven: Yale University Press, 1985.

Reiss, Stephen. *City Games: The Evolution of American Urban Society and the Rise of Sports*. Urbana: University of Illinois Press, 1989.

———, ed. *The American Sporting Experience: A Historical Anthology of Sport in America*. New York: Leisure Press, 1984.

Rotman, Brian. *Signifying Nothing: The Semiotics of Zero*. Stanford: Stanford University Press, 1987.

Schivelbusch, Wolfgang. *The Railway Journey: The Industrialization of Time and Space in the Nineteenth Century*. Berkeley: University of California Press, 1986.

Schwartz, Vanessa R. *Spectacular Realities: Early Mass Culture in Fin-de-Siècle Paris*. Berkeley: University of California Press, 1997.

Shiff, Richard. "The End of Impressionism." In *The New Painting: Impressionism, 1874–1886*. San Francisco: Fine Arts Museums of San Francisco, 1986.

———. *Cézanne and the End of Impressionism*. Chicago: University of Chicago Press, 1984.

Smith, Gary, ed. *Benjamin: Philosophy, Aesthetics, History*. Chicago: University of Chicago Press, 1989.

Somers, Dale. *The Rise of Sports in New Orleans, 1850–1900*. Baton Rouge: Louisiana State University Press, 1972.

Tichi, Cecelia. *Shifting Gears: Technology, Literature, Culture in Modernist America*. Chapel Hill: University of North Carolina Press, 1987.

Weiskel, Thomas. *The Romantic Sublime: Studies in the Structure and Psychology of Transcendence.* Baltimore: Johns Hopkins University Press, 1976.

Williams, Linda. *Figures of Desire: A Theory and Analysis of Surrealist Film.* Berkeley: University of California Press, 1981.

———. "Film Body: An Implantation of Perversions." In *Narrative, Apparatus, Ideology,* ed. Philip Rosen. New York: Columbia University Press, 1986.

Index

Leo Charney teaches film studies at the University of New
Mexico. He is coeditor (with Vanessa R. Schwartz) of
Cinema and the Invention of Modern Life.
Library of Congress Cataloging-in-Publication Data
Charney, Leo.
Empty moments : cinema, modernity, and drift / Leo Charney.
Includes bibliographical references and index.
ISBN 0-8223-2076-2 (cloth : alk. paper).
ISBN 0-8223-2090-8 (pbk. : alk. paper)
1. Motion pictures—Philosophy.   I. Title.
PN1995.C4475 1998
791.43′01—dc21   97-41661 CIP